T0150567

ANOTHER EUROPE?

AFTER THE THIRD NO

To the peoples of Europe

ANOTHER EUROPE?

The Conversations of Publia and Lydia

AFTER THE THIRD NO

THE LILLIPUT PRESS
DUBLIN

First published 2008 by
THE LILLIPUT PRESS
62–63 Sitric Road, Arbour Hill
Dublin 7, Ireland
www.lilliputpress.ie

Copyright © LSE Mackinder Programme 2008

ISBN 978 1 84351 150 2

1 3 5 7 9 10 8 6 4 2

A CIP record for this title is available
from The British Library.

Set in 12.5 pt on 15 pt Perpetua by Marsha Swan
Printed in Ireland by ColourBooks of Dublin

Contents

After an unequivocal experience of the inefficiency of the subsisting federal government, you are called upon to deliberate on a new Constitution for the United States of America. The subject speaks its own importance; comprehending in its consequences nothing less than the existence of the UNION, the safety and welfare of the parts of which it is composed, the fate of an empire in many respects the most interesting in the world. It has been frequently remarked that it seems to have been reserved to the people of this country, by their conduct and example, to decide the important question, whether societies of men are really capable or not of establishing good government from reflection and choice, or whether they are forever destined to depend for their political constitutions on accident and force. If there be any truth in the remark, the crisis at which we are arrived may with propriety be regarded as the era in which that decision is to be made; and a wrong election of the part we shall act may, in this view, deserve to be considered as the general misfortune of mankind.

ALEXANDER HAMILTON – as 'PUBLIUS'
(General Introduction, *Federalist* No. 1, 1787)

A popular Government without popular information or the means of acquiring it, is but a Prologue to a Farce or a Tragedy or perhaps both. Knowledge will forever govern ignorance; and a people who mean to be their own governors must arm themselves with the power that knowledge gives.

JAMES MADISON
(Letter to W.T Barry, 4 August 1822)

Preface

Why was it suggested that in the 1940s rural Irish policemen and their bicycles came to resemble each other in character and in behaviour? In Flann O'Brien's famous surrealist novel, *The Third Policeman*, it is the third policeman himself who explains. The Atomic Theory tells why policemen prop up the bar stiffly like bicycles leaning against the wall. It is an atomic theory – but not as physicists know it. The Third Policeman's theory is that because of the long hours that the policeman and his bicycle spend in close proximity to each other, an exchange of atoms occurs between them. So the policeman becomes part bicycle and the bicycle, part policeman.

Jean Monnet, the father of the European Union, had a somewhat similar expectation of how the relationship between the people of Europe and the political project of 'ever closer union' would develop. Over time, generation by generation, the new European identity would seep into the people as a result of close and growing proximity. But it hasn't turned out like that. The project for a European Constitution has experienced 'no' votes in France and the Netherlands in 2005 – the First and Second

No's – and has now received The Third No in Ireland in 2008. As well as being a rejection of the main party elements of Ireland's political settlement since Independence, the decisive Irish 'No' in the referendum on the Lisbon Treaty on 12 June 2008 contained one fact which documented how Monnet's version of the Third Policeman's Atomic Theory has gone awry. Irish voters under 28 years of age voted 'No' in a ratio of 2:1.

These letters of Publia, which record her conversations with her friend Lydia, are the first product of a research project into the deeper trends animating recent, tumultuous and confusing events in European affairs of which the Third No is the most recent. The great French historian, Fernand Braudel, famously remarked that one could not hope to make sense of the agitated oscillations of the waves across the ocean surface by observing them only where they are to be seen. One had to dive below the surface to study the driving currents. Just so: 'event history' is connected to the longer wave-lengths of the cultural, moral and religious as much as to the economic, material and geopolitical dimensions of history. The relationship is not deterministic; but the surface history of events can only admit to shallow insight in its own terms alone, lacking those simultaneous connections to many subjects and disciplines.

The Mackinder Programme for the Study of Long Wave Events at the London School of Economics and Political Science undertook this work in order to help deepen public understanding of why the current travails, admitted and not admitted, of the European project have come about. As the primary research proceeded, it became plain that a conventional form of academic report would not best serve the public scholarship to which the Programme is dedicated. Hence, the composition of these letters. The academic report appears with other supporting materials on the web-site associated with this book (www.anothereurope.eu).

Insofar as any single individual event can be credited for the inspiration to invite Publia to take up her pen to record her conversations with her friend Lydia, that event was the clear-cut rejections of the draft EU constitution in the French and Dutch referenda of 2005 – the First and Second No's. The striking difference between the general public view expressed in France and the Netherlands and the subsequent response by politicians throughout Europe suggested, at the least, fundamental irreconcilabilities between diverging visions of Europe's future: issues as momentous as those which confronted the American Republic in 1787. In that year, James Madison, Alexander Hamilton and John Jay together summonsed 'Publius' to help persuade the citizens of New York of the virtues of the United States' Constitution of 1787 through the medium of *The Federalist Papers*.

At this time of evidently deep-seated disagreement about what to do next in Europe, it therefore seemed logical to look to this stirring example of public scholarship. So the idea formed that the Mackinder Programme's project might most responsibly fulfill its duty by inviting Publius' sister and her friend, Lydia, to present and debate their respective visions on Europe both in principle, as well as issue by issue.

The Letters are written to be internally self-sufficient. There is therefore an occasional element of repetition, which permits the reading of any single letter without presuming knowledge of any other. The Letters are offered, as Publia herself writes in her Preamble, as a contribution to debate on momentous decisions facing all of us as Europeans. There are serious judgements to be made, notably about whether, in Publia's words, 'yesterday's radical visions can meet today's political realities'. The views attributed here to the two ladies will probably not be found displayed by any single person in quite this comprehensive fashion. But their dialogue exposes the only two logically

consistent routes open to the building of a democratically legitimate, popular and hence viable Europe, at the same time making plain the essential cultural, moral and political prerequisites
for success in either case.

This has been an undertaking of many hands and minds.
Especially, the contribution of distinguished thinkers and prac-
titioners across Europe and across the spectrum of opinion
about the European Union who kindly agreed to be interviewed
is gratefully acknowledged. The book is therefore genuinely a
fusion of thinking and, to register this aspect of the enterprise,
the names of those who assisted are listed after this Preface and
before Publia takes up her pen.

All interviews were conducted with an undertaking of con-
fidentiality given to the interviewee that is respected in this
work; in due course, the formal paper presenting the materials
arising from the research interviews will appear initially on the
anothereurope.eu website. There is, of course, no presumption
that any individual endorses any or all of the text that we have
now produced. But the conversations between Publia and Lydia
have been closely constructed from the raw materials of those
many, very varied interviews. So, if interviewees read carefully,
they may privately find their own arguments and phrases in the
mouths of one or other of these ladies!

The other acknowledgment that is inextricable from the
first is to Ms Johanna Möhring, the formidably multilingual and
hard-working Research Officer of this project. Without her
meticulous conduct of the interviews, subsequent collation and
creative transformation of the material, Lydia and Publia would
not have found their voices in the way that they do.

Ms Möhring was ably supported in the tasks of transcrip-
tion and translation by Miss Alison Suter, who has assisted me
in all my work for many years. We are also grateful for detailed
critique and drafting advice received from a wide range of

colleagues as the conversations and letters developed. Staff at
Wilton Park, the Foreign Office's independent conference centre, were immensely helpful in identifying some key interviewees for us from their unrivalled range of contacts. The LSE is
grateful to the Smith Richardson Foundation for financial support of the project.

It is to be hoped that the conversations of Publia and Lydia
can assist the reader both to escape the limiting and often trivial-
izing terms in which debate about European issues is often cast
and to come to judgements that are settled upon solid historical
and philosophical foundations which are themselves part of the
bedrock of European culture and thought. It could not be more
appropriate that *Another Europe?* is first published in Ireland at
the moment when the country is the very fulcrum of European
debate between the two views of Europe's future given voice
through Publia and Lydia and set out as plainly and as systemati-
cally as we can – and for the first time – in this book.

G. Prins
Director   *London*
LSE Mackinder Programme   *June 2008*

Acknowledgments

Mr Urban Ahlin (Sweden), former Chairman of the Foreign Relations Committee of the Swedish Parliament; foreign policy spokesperson for the Social Democratic Party and Deputy Chair of the Foreign Relations Committee, Stockholm

Mr Peter Altmaier (Germany), MP, Parliamentary Secretary of State, Ministry of Interior, Berlin

Dr Giuliano Amato (Italy), former Prime Minister and former Vice-Chairman of the Praesidium of the European Convention; former Minister of the Interior, Rome

Professor Dr Leszek Balcerowicz (Poland), former Deputy Prime Minister and Minister of Finance; former President of the National Bank of Poland (NBP); Professor of Economics at the Warsaw School of Economics (WSE), Warsaw

Mr Rafael L. Bardají (Spain), former National Security Advisor, Director of International Policy, Foundation for Social Research and Analysis (FAES); Senior Adviser to former Spanish Prime Minister José María Aznar, Madrid

Dr Lorenzo Bini Smaghi (Italy), Member of the Executive Board of the
European Central Bank (ECB), Frankfurt, Germany

Mr Frits Bolkestein (The Netherlands), former Leader of the People's Party for Freedom and Democracy ('Volkspartij voor Vrijheid
en Democratie', VVD); former EU Commissioner for Internal Market,
Taxation and Customs Union; Professor at the universities of Leiden
and Delft, Amsterdam

Ms Emma Bonino (Italy), former European Commissioner responsible
for Consumer Policy, Consumer Health, Food Safety and Fisheries, as
well as the European Community Humanitarian Office (ECHO); former
MEP; former Minister for International Trade and European Affairs; Vice
President of the Senate, Rome

Professor Frédéric Bozo (France), Professor of Contemporary History,
Sorbonne (University of Paris 3, Department of European Studies)

Sir Colin Budd (Great Britain), Chair of the Liberal Democrats' Europe
Policy Working Group, London

Ms Signe Burgstaller (Sweden), Director and Deputy Head of Department,
Security Policy Department, Ministry for Foreign Affairs, Stockholm

Dr Lucio Caracciolo (Italy), Editor in Chief, Geopolitical Review *Limes*
and Eurasian Review of Geopolitics *Heartland*, Rome

Mr Robert Cooper (Great Britain), former Head of Policy Planning Staff
at the British Foreign Office; Director-General, External and Politico-
Military Affairs, Council of the European Union, Brussels, Belgium

Dr Marta Dassù (Italy), former foreign policy adviser to the Prime Minister of Italy (1998–2001); General Director, International Programs,
Aspen Institute Italia, Editor of *Aspenia*, Rome

Mr Joël Decaillon (France), Confederal Secretary, European Trade
Union Confederation (ETUC), Brussels, Belgium

Mr Pierre Defraigne (Belgium), former Deputy Director-General of EC

Directorate-General Trade; Director, Eur-Ifri, Brussels-based branch of the French Institute of International Relations (IFRI) in Paris

Mr Philippe de Buck (Belgium), Secretary-General, BUSINESS-EUROPE (The Confederation of European Business), Brussels

Dr Álvaro de Vasconcelos (Portugal), Director, European Union Institute for Security Studies (ISS), Paris, France

Mr Rob de Wijk (The Netherlands), former Head of the Defence Concepts Division of the Netherlands Ministry of Defence; Director, The Hague Centre for Strategic Studies (HCSS), The Hague; Professor of Strategic Studies, Leiden University

Baroness Mia Doornaert (Belgium), Diplomatic Editor, *De Standaard*; former President of the International Federation of Journalists, Brussels

Mr Peter Dun (Great Britain), Adviser, European Commission, Brussels, Belgium

Professor Julian Lindley-French (Great Britain), Head of Military Operational Science (Royal Military Academy of Netherlands); Senior Associate Fellow, Defence Academy of the UK

Mr Roland Freudenstein (Germany), former Director of the Warsaw branch of the Konrad Adenauer Foundation; Director, Joint Representation of the Free and Hanseatic City of Hamburg and the State of Schleswig-Holstein to the European Union, Brussels, Belgium

Dr Susan George (United States/France), author *We, the Peoples of Europe*; Vice-President of ATTAC France for six years; Chair of the Planning Board of the Transnational Institute in Amsterdam, Paris, France

Dr Ulrike Guérot (Germany), Senior Research Fellow and Head of the Berlin Office, European Council on Foreign Relations, Berlin

Mr Sverker Gustavsson (Sweden), Professor, Department of Government, Uppsala University; Chairman of the Swedish network for European Studies in Political Science, Uppsala

Mr Hans Hækkerup (Denmark), former Minister of Defence and UN Under-Secretary-General serving as Special Representative of the Secretary-General/Head of UN Interim Administration in Kosovo; China Studies Research Director, Institute of Strategy, Royal Danish Defence College, Copenhagen

Dr Vladimír Handl (Czech Republic), Research Fellow, Institute of International Relations, Prague

Mr Jean Heinrich (France), Lieutenant General (ret.), French Army; former Head of Military Intelligence; President, Supervisory Committee, GEOS, Montrouge

Dr Philippe Herzog (France), former MEP; President, 'Confrontations Europe'; member of the Economic Advisory Council of the Prime Minister, Paris

Professor Bertel Heurlin (Denmark), Jean Monnet Professor of European Security and Integration, University of Copenhagen; Chairman of the Danish Institute for Military Studies, Copenhagen

Dr Jonathan Holslag (Belgium), Research Director, Institute of Contemporary China Studies, Vrije Universiteit Brussel, Brussels

Mr Gints Jegermanis (Latvia), Head of Policy Planning, Foreign Ministry, Riga

Ms Christina Jutterström (Sweden), former Editor in Chief of *Dagens Nyheter* and of *Expressen*; former CEO of Swedish Television, Author of *Free Television? – Public Service in a New Mediaworld*, Stockholm

Dr Jan Karlas (Czech Republic), Director of Studies, Institute of International Relations, Prague

Dr Petr Kratochvíl (Czech Republic), Deputy Director, Institute of International Relations, Prague

Dr Riina Ruth Kionka (Estonia), former Undersecretary for EU Affairs and Ambassador to Germany; Personal Representative of the EU

Secretary-General/High Representative Javier Solana for Human Rights, Brussels, Belgium

Mr Tom Kremer (Great Britain), Author, *The Missing Heart of Europe*

Professor Dr Horst Günter Krenzler (Germany), former Director-General for External Relations at the European Commission; Counsel at Freshfields Bruckhaus Deringer, Brussels, Belgium; Professor, Institute for International Law, University of Munich, Munich

Lord Leach (Great Britain), Author, *Europe: A Concise Encyclopedia*; Director, Jardine Matheson Holdings

Mr Christian Leffler (Sweden), Head, Cabinet of Vice President Margot Wallström, European Commission, Brussels, Belgium

Mr Matti Maasikas (Estonia), Secretary-General, Ministry of Foreign Affairs, Tallinn

Mr Emile H. Malet (France), Director and Editor, Journal *Passages*, Paris

Ms Jette Elbæk Maressa (Denmark), Foreign editor of *Jyllands-Posten*, Copenhagen

Dr Andreas Maurer (Germany), former Adviser to the European Convention; Head of Research Unit 'European Integration', German Institute for International and Security Affairs ('Stiftung Wissenschaft und Politik'), Berlin

Professor Dr Dr Peter-Christian Müller-Graff (Germany), Director, Institute for Economic Law and European Law, University of Heidelberg; former Adviser to the European Convention; Honorary Jean Monnet Professor, Heidelberg

Mr Andrés Ortega (Spain), former Adviser to the then Spanish Prime Minister Felipe González, editorial writer and columnist at *El País*; Editor of the Spanish-language edition of *Foreign Policy*, Madrid

Professor Dr Žaneta Ozoliņa (Latvia), Chairperson, Strategic Analysis

Commission under the auspices of the President of the Republic of Latvia; Head, Department of Political Science, Faculty of Social Sciences, University of Latvia, Riga

Professor Dr Jean-Jacques Rosa (France), Professor of Economics, Paris Institute of Political Studies ('Institut d'Etudes Politiques de Paris', IEP), Paris

Dr Alexander Schaub (Germany), former Director-General for Internal Market and Services and Director-General for Competition at the European Commission; Counsel at Freshfields Bruckhaus Deringer, Brussels, Belgium

Mr Guillaume Schlumberger (France), Director, Foundation for Research Strategy ('Fondation pour la Recherche Stratégique'), Paris

Mr Jiří Schneider (Czech Republic), former Political Director of the Ministry of Foreign Affairs of the Czech Republic; Programme Director, Prague Security Studies Institute, Prague

Dr Pedro Schwartz (Spain), Professor Extraordinary of San Pablo CEU University and of St Louis University in Madrid; Board Member of the Centre for European Policy Studies, Brussels, Madrid

Professor Roger Scruton (Great Britain), former Professor of Aesthetics at Birkbeck College, London; former Professor of Philosophy and University Professor at Boston University; Research Professor at the Institute for the Psychological Sciences, Arlington, VA, USA

Ms Monika Sie Dhian Ho (The Netherlands), former Senior Researcher of the Scientific Council for Government Policy, The Hague; Director of the Wiardi Beckman Foundation (think tank of the Dutch Labour Party), Amsterdam

Professor Larry Siedentop (Great Britain), Emeritus Fellow of Keble College; former Faculty Lecturer in Political Thought, University of Oxford, England

Dr Stefano Silvestri (Italy), former Adviser to the Prime Minister, the

Minister of Internal Affairs, the Minister of Industry and Trade and the Minister of Defence; former Under Secretary of State for Defence; President, Institute of International Affairs ('Istituto Affari Internazionali'), Rome

Dr Aleksander Smolar (Poland), former Chief Adviser to Tadeusz Mazowiecki, the first post-communist, democratically elected Prime Minister of Poland; former Foreign Adviser to the Prime Minister Hanna Suchocka; President, Stefan Batory Foundation, Warsaw

Mr Klaus-Dieter Sohn (Germany), Policy Analyst, Employment and Social Security and Equality of Treatment, Centrum für Europäische Politik, Freiburg

Dr Klaus-Heinrich Standke (Germany), former Director for Science and Technology at the United Nations; President, Committee for French-German-Polish Cooperation – Weimar Triangle, Berlin-Paris-Warsaw, Berlin

Ms Dana Spinant (Romania), Editor, *European Voice*, Brussels, Belgium

Ms Gisela Stuart (Germany/Great Britain), former Health Minister; former British Labour Party representative on the European Convention and member of its Praesidium; MP, Birmingham Edgbaston

Mr Pavel Telička (Czech Republic), former Chief Negotiator for the accession of the Czech Republic to the European Union; former Ambassador and Head of Czech Mission to the EU; former EU Commissioner; Partner, BXL Consulting, Brussels, Belgium – Prague

Mr Carl Tham (Sweden), former Minister of Education and Science; former Swedish Ambassador to Germany; former Director-General of the Swedish International Development Co-Operation Agency (SIDA); Adviser, The Workers' Educational Association, Stockholm

Professor Dr José Ignacio Torreblanca (Spain), former Senior Analyst for EU affairs, Elcano Royal Institute for International Affairs; Senior Research Fellow and Head of the Madrid Office, European Council on Foreign Relations, Madrid

Baron Franciskus van Daele (Belgium), former Ambassador and Permanent Representative to the European Union; former Ambassador to the United States; Ambassador and Permanent Representative of Belgium to NATO, Brussels

Dr Peter van Ham (The Netherlands), Director of Global Governance Research, Netherlands Institute of International Relations 'Clingendael'; Professor, College of Europe in Bruges, Belgium, The Hague

Mr Frank van Kappen (The Netherlands), Major General (ret.), Royal Netherlands Marine Corps; Adviser, The Hague Centre for Strategic Studies (HCSS), The Hague

Dr Bert Van Roosebeke (Germany), Policy Analyst Internal Market, Centrum für Europäische Politik, Freiburg

Professor Dr Roland Vaubel (Germany), Professor of Economics, University of Mannheim; Member of the European Constitutional Group, Mannheim

Ms Anne Mette Vestergaard (Denmark), Head of Department, EU Coordination, Ministry of Foreign Affairs, Copenhagen

Dr Edmund Peter Wellenstein (The Netherlands), former Secretary-General of the High Authority of the European Coal and Steel Community; former Director-General for External Relations of the European Commission, The Hague

Professor Dr Wolfgang Wessels (Germany), Jean Monnet Chair for European Affairs, University of Cologne; Chair, Institute for European Policy, Berlin; Chair of the Trans European Policy Studies Association, Brussels, Cologne

Preamble

These letters are addressed to the people of Europe, and concern the future of Europe. They express the thoughts of a sincere European, one who endorses the commonality of the European nations, recognizing in Europe and its civilization one of the great achievements of mankind. Like the 'Publius' of the *Federalist Papers*, she is addressing a people to whom she belongs, whose destiny she shares, and whose hopes and fears she knows from within as her own. She has no axe to grind, no specific national agenda to advance, and no ambitions to rival those of politicians who have been instrumental in shaping the European project from its modest origins to its present dominance.

The event that triggered the writing of these letters was the unequivocal rejection in 2005 of the proposed Constitutional Treaty by the people of France and the Netherlands. I remember the occasion well. My friend Lydia and I were sitting in her favourite restaurant in the *Campo dei Fiori* in Rome when we heard the dramatic news of the Dutch rejection, coming hard on the heels of the French 'non': nearly two-thirds of two-thirds of the electorate of one of the six founding signatories of

the Treaty of Rome. I had been lamenting the disappearance of
the peasant vendors, whose vegetables used to be brought here
each morning from the *campagna*; lamenting the loss of those
little shops marked *Vini ed Olii* where cool wine from the Fra-
scati hills issued from nickel-plated taps set in walls of marble;
lamenting the disappearance of those puffy wads of Italian currency, the value of which declined in your handbag, but which
were such a vivid symbol of a country where trust is vested in
the people you know, and never in something with official print
on it.

Lydia dismissed my lamentations with a wave of the hand.
'Those things', she said, 'were the by-products of an economy
that was bound to disappear. You don't survive in the world as
it is by retreating to vanished forms of economic life. You go
forward and embrace the future, and that means embracing the
European Union, which has done more to stabilize the Italian
economy than any Italian government since Marcus Aurelius.'

In normal circumstances, I would not have raised the subject
of our deeper disagreement. However, it was this profoundly
democratic moment in Europe's affairs which prompted the
re-opening between us of a once intense dialogue on the European project. In those heady, distant days of 1968 when we first
met as students at the Sorbonne, it was an idea rich in promise and expectation for all of us. Both of us are the offspring
of mixed parentage, she German and French, I Scottish and
Czech. Many cups of coffee stand witness to the extended conversations across the years that had revealed an ever-widening
gap between us, to the point where silence became the protector of a friendship reaching back to our youth. But the shock of
the unexpected turn of events reopened a discussion we both
thought long exhausted.

It was in Rome, then, that I proposed to Lydia the idea of
revisiting the conversations of our youth in the light of these

much-changed times. My idea was to examine anew each sphere of the European project. I wanted us to explore together what were its objectives, achievements, costs and prospects. I thought that such an exercise would be as much of interest and profit to her as I knew that it was to me. As together we grappled with our inquiry, her great passion for European unity and her intimate professional contacts with the leaders engaged in the construction of the European Union proved to be valuable assets.

The idea of European integration was conceived during the First World War, became a political reality in the wake of the Second, and is marked by the conflicts that gave birth to it. It seemed reasonable, even imperative, in 1950 to bring the nations of Europe together in a way that would prevent the wars that had twice almost destroyed the continent. And because conflicts breed radicalism, the new Europe was conceived as a comprehensive plan – one that would eliminate the sources of European conflict, and place cooperation rather than competition at the heart of the continental order. The architects of the plan had little in common apart from a belief in European civilization and a distrust of the nation state. The *éminence grise,* Jean Monnet, was a transnational bureaucrat, inspired by the vision of a united Europe in which war would be a thing of the past. His friend and colleague at the League of Nations, the Englishman Arthur Salter, wrote a book in 1931 – *The United States of Europe* – which set out that shared vision in detail. His close collaborator, Walter Hallstein, was an academic German technocrat, who believed in international jurisdiction as the natural successor to the laws of the nation states. Monnet, Salter and Hallstein were joined by Altiero Spinelli, a romantic communist who advocated a United States of Europe legitimized by a democratically elected European Parliament. Such people were not isolated enthusiasts, but part of a broad movement among the post-war European elites with initial strong support among the war-weary nations. They sought and obtained the support of popular political leaders like Konrad Adenauer, Robert Schuman and Alcide De Gasperi to translate their ideas into concrete political form. The creation of the European Coal and Steel Community (ECSC – the Schuman Plan) in 1951 was the initial step in the realization of a much more ambitious project that would acquire legitimacy, they reasoned, if it could first be accepted in this circumscribed form.

I do not wish to disparage the efforts of those public-spirited people. We should remember that, when the first instruments of European cooperation were being devised, our continent was divided by the Iron Curtain, with half of Germany and all of the central and eastern European countries under Soviet occupation, and fascist regimes installed in Portugal and Spain. France was in constant turmoil, with a Communist Party commanding the support of almost a third of its electorate. The free remnant of Europe was critically dependent upon the Atlantic alliance, and the marks of occupation and defeat were apparent throughout the continent. Only radical measures, it seemed, could restore political, moral and economic health, and those measures were intended to replace the old antagonisms with a new spirit of friendship. As a result, European integration was conceived in uni-directional terms, as a process of ever-increasing *unity*. Each increase in central power was to be matched by a diminution of national power. Every summit, each regulation and Directive added to the *acquis communautaire* has since carried within itself this specific equation.

We have undeniably gained much since those days. Material prosperity, security from external threat, longevity and health are now taken for granted. And those benefits have certainly been furthered by international cooperation – by the North Atlantic Treaty Organization (NATO), by the GATT (General Agreement on Tariffs and Trade (now superseded by the World

Trade Organization – WTO), with the European institutions
having had an important part to play. By providing stable links
to the surrounding world, they have facilitated the democrati-
zation of countries previously subject to fascist or communist
dictatorship. By fostering trade and exchange among its members and by giving a prominent international role to France
and Germany, they have stabilized those two countries, both
internally and externally.

However, since then, conditions in the world at large and
especially in Europe have radically changed. The instruments
for dealing with the problems of 50 years ago are not necessarily adapted to the demands of today. The Soviet Union has
collapsed and has left a legacy of political distrust and covert
lawlessness in its former European satellites. The constraints
imposed by the European Union, well intentioned as they may
have been, made the continent less able to adapt to the challenges of a world economy in the throes of immense change.
Europe's rapidly diminishing share of global trade and wealth
speaks of a shift in power of a kind that is only seen every few
centuries. Mass immigrations from Africa, Asia and the Middle East have created potentially inassimilable minorities in the
hearts of France, Germany, Holland, Spain, Italy and Britain.
There is a spiritual vacuum in Europe into which materialism
and many enthusiasms have flowed without hindrance. The
population is getting older and sparser. Information technology
has created a virtual world where geographical boundaries have
lost much of their significance. Religious strife, and uncondi-
tional terrorism in general, are posing dangers that cannot be
anticipated and met within a structure that was once visionary.

The question these letters will attempt to answer is to what
extent yesterday's radical visions can meet today's political
needs. Can the simple formula of creating an ever more powerful central body, at the expense of diminishing the authority of

the nation state and eroding the role of national parliaments, work in changed circumstances? For whatever our vision of Europe's future, in the present we shall have to depend on the nation state for its realization. The nation states are not equally stable, equally democratic, equally free or equally obedient to the rule of law. But they are all we have. They alone inspire the loyalty and obedience of the European people, and without them there is no way that the machinery of the Union can work. To what extent can any process which aims to weaken diversity and to supplant those motive forces tap the true resources and the creative potential of our people, and revitalize the idea of European civilization?

There are themes which resonate like a drumbeat through these letters. One is the doctrine of 'subsidiarity'. This word, incorporated into the Maastricht Treaty, is a term of Roman Catholic theology. Here, 'subsidiarity' means that decisions are taken always at the lowest level compatible with the over-arching authority of the Church, which is asserted only in those rare cases where the Christian community as a whole is in need of guidance. The term was appropriated by Wilhelm Röpke, the German economist, who, exiled from Nazi Germany in Switzerland, was amazed and impressed to discover a society which was the opposite in so many ways to the one from which he had escaped. Swiss society is organized from the bottom up, and resolves its problems at the local level. It acts through the free association of citizens, in those 'little platoons' to which Edmund Burke had made such passionate appeal when decrying the top-down dictatorship of the French Revolution. Subsidiarity, in this understanding of the term, refers to the right of local communities to take decisions for themselves, including the decision to surrender the matter to a larger forum. It is the way to reconcile a market economy with the local loyalties and public spirit that it might otherwise erode.

Röpke was a true European, a thinker for whom the sovereignty of the individual and the pursuit of the common good form an indissoluble unity. He endorsed the early efforts at post-war cooperation, while urging the architects of the new institutions to follow the path of 'subsidiarity' rather than that of centralized power. A humane and intelligent economist and a liberal social thinker, he was also, like his friend Ludwig Erhard, Konrad Adenauer's economy minister and successor as chancellor, a believer in open and accountable government. He advocated subsidiarity as the *sine qua non* of popular sovereignty, the way to ensure that powers would be passed always upwards from the bottom, and that those at the top would remain answerable to those beneath them.

In the European Union (EU) as it is today, the term 'subsidiarity' takes on an altogether different meaning. It denotes the means whereby powers are allocated from the top. It is the EU and its institutions that decide where subsidiary powers begin and end. For the Union, national governments are autonomous only at the 'subsidiary' level, with the European institutions uniquely empowered to determine which level that is. The two interpretations of 'subsidiarity' are, of course, incompatible. I believe that Röpke's understanding is more profound. Lydia, on the other hand, is convinced of the need for central authority and a top-down approach. The letters will seek to draw out the diverse implications for Europe of following one or the other course.

The other constant theme running through the letters is the tension between unity and diversity. Aware of this dichotomy, and appreciating the obstacle it posed to the objective of 'ever closer union', the Brussels wordsmiths coined a new motto: 'Unity through Diversity'. Mottos do not resolve genuine differences. The difficulties encountered by Lydia and her friends determined to integrate Europe lie precisely in the excessive diversity of the continent's nations, their social and political culture, their laws and ways of doing business, their languages and customs, the depth of their democracy. When you integrate, as the origin of the word suggests, you are pouring what was many into one. And when you operate from the centre, top-down, the way you go about it is by making rules and regulations that apply uniformly throughout the continent. The question, therefore, is how far to impose such uniformity. How far is it possible? How far is it useful?

Unlike Publius, when he wrote the *Federalist Papers*, the author of these letters has before her no such constitutional model as he had, and therefore labours under a disadvantage from which Publius did not suffer. But she has the advantage of being able to look back at 50 years of European history. Does the EU, as currently structured, provide what the people have a right to expect in the matter of cooperation between neighbours? Are there other, perhaps more viable, alternatives for the nations of Europe to work together? By sharing this record of my conversations with Lydia, my hope is to resuscitate debate; for debate is the only sure protection of tolerance and therefore of democracy. So, let us debate the future of our continent in terms that accord with the reality of the 21st century.

European Identity

In my many and varied conversations on the future of the European continent with my long-standing friend Lydia, the subject of European identity has been never far from the surface. Both of us believe that a European identity, worthy of being nourished and protected, exists. But the two of us have rather different views about its content and meaning. Being an enthusiastic supporter of the great European unification project, Lydia tends to highlight the close emotional bonds that tie us together as Europeans. On one occasion, she cited a rather lyrical passage of George Steiner's attributing the instinctive feeling of being European to the fact that Europe had been built at a human echelon, traversable from north to south and east to west on foot, to its culture of cafés inviting discussion and debate, to its presence in history all around us, to the naming of streets and places after European statesmen, artists and philosophers. She stressed that belonging to Europe was felt most strongly precisely when people were missing its actual presence, in countries cast adrift by the cruelties of history, by wars and dictatorships, yearning to be reunited with the European family, sometimes for centuries.

Having this sense of being European close to my heart, I feel a great deal of empathy with what she is saying, especially since it is patently impossible to build a great European project if the peoples do not feel committed to it. On the other hand, one cannot deny that the stability of the whole, the very treaties which form the EU are dependent on the nation states, states that are in turn reliant on the sense of national identity felt by their people. Lydia always seems somewhat irritated by the mention of 'nation'. 'Look,' she said, 'people do not have only one identity. One and the same woman is European, French and a Toulousienne. Which of those identities is important to her will depend upon the situation in which she needs to express it. In the matter of rugby she will support Toulouse against Nîmes; in the matter of agricultural subsidies she will support France against Britain; but in the large issues of global politics she will experience herself as a European, heir to the specific form of life that has shaped our continent. We need the institutions that will express that form of life, and defend it against the entropic forces of globalization and fanaticism. That was the purpose of the European Union, and it is a purpose that remains.'

Even so, all the cases adduced by Lydia are examples of multiple identities that do not compete. When it comes to defending one's territory, paying taxes to help one's kith and kin, delegating powers to a government and other such matters of political import, history demonstrates that national identity not only competes with a European one, it takes precedence over it. Lydia's response to this observation is interesting: 'Identity is not a static concept, it evolves. We are shaped by emotional and symbolic experience, something that has unfor- tunately been rather lacking at the European level. While Euro- pean integration itself has contributed to the formation of a distinct European identity, the peoples of Europe simply have not been Europeanized yet. Socialization of our young generation – today's children – is the leading task of this century. If we can succeed, then they will have no personal memory of any other reality; only folk memory. So, we have to promote a strong European identity by investing in education, breaking down the barriers of school and university *curricula* and ending national navel-gazing. In dark hours, I sometimes fear that the drive, the emotions in favour of Europe, are gone. For the next generation, it is an unconscious *fait accompli*. It must be made conscious for them. Therefore, we must urgently create a European public space, a key element in the construction of Europe with the help of truly European media. Strengthening European security and defence policy is a means to foster Europe's identity. Joint fighting and dying form strong bonds. If we want integration to proceed, we depend on the existence of such a shared identity to invest our common European institutions with the trust they deserve.'

When I asked her what exactly was this European identity, and how well it was captured by the institutions erected in its name, Lydia mostly talked about a feeling of belonging to a civilization built on human ideas. 'You, Publia, would surely agree that we are all children of both Athens and Jerusalem, on a constant quest for nobility of spirit and human dignity throughout the ages, with the arts, the humanities, philosophy and theology to guide us? Creative friction between our Greek roots founded in rationality and our longing for spirituality has made us who we are today. This civilization has always been European in the sense that its spirit has transcended national boundaries. It has been driven by constant cross-border intellectual exchange. Yes, it is true, it is carried mostly by an elite. The peoples of Europe have been left to identify with national cultures, exposed only to a very compartmentalized version of the European spirit. This spirit is the force that is driving European integration.'

The high seriousness of Lydia's tone came to me as no
surprise. It brought back memories of our earnest debates in
the Café de Flore on the Boulevard Saint-Germain, the place
infused with that heady mixture of the rhetoric and the ciga-
rette smoke of Sartre, de Beauvoir and the existentialist movement of our youth. I replied in this manner:

'There is no dispute between us in the realization that
Europe is not just a geographical region – not even a geographical region – but a civilization that grew from Roman imperial
government and the Christian Church, and took on its distinc-
tively modern form in the wake of the Enlightenment. We are
individuals, responsible for our own lives, and answerable to
judgement. Our lives are lived in two spheres, the private and
the public. To the first belong the choices and values which
shape our individual destinies. To the second sphere belong the
laws and institutions that permit the peaceful growth of society.
Religion belongs in the first of these spheres: it may be, and
perhaps ought to be, acknowledged in the public realm, but is
not the source of public order. This separation of spheres was
laid down by Jesus himself, in the parable of the Tribute Money,
was taken up by the early Church, with the 'two swords' doctrine of Pope Gelasius I, and acknowledged in the long conflicts
between Pope and Emperor, church and state, which ended with
the final triumph of secular government at the Enlightenment.
This history is integral to the European experience. It informs
our sense of the individual as both morally autonomous and
publicly responsible, free to realize his conception of the good
in private, but obedient in public to laws that guarantee the
freedom of others. Equally important is the Judaeo-Christian
morality that is summarized not in the Ten Commandments,
but in the brilliant précis of Leviticus: 'Thou shalt love the Lord
thy God with all thy heart and with all thy soul and with all thy
mind and with all thy strength, and thou shalt love thy neigh-

bour as thyself.' Translated into modern idiom, the commandments correspond to the two spheres of human life. In the first
– the sphere of what we are for ourselves – we are dedicated
to the highest good. In the second – the sphere of what we
are for others – we are bound by the principle of neighbour
love. The second principle was re-formulated at the Enlightenment by Kant as the categorical imperative: to act only on
that maxim which you can will as a law for all mankind and to
treat humanity, whether in yourself or in another, never as a
means only but always as an end in itself. And both principles
are brought together in the prayer on which Europeans from
time immemorial have been raised, which asks God to 'forgive
us our trespasses as we forgive those who trespass against us'. It
is surely plausible to suggest that the two Commandments and
the Lord's Prayer form the moral, spiritual and emotional foundation of the thing that comes naturally to Europeans, namely
recognition of the Other as other than yourself?'

We are commanded to love our enemy, to pursue forgive-
ness and to accept the rule of secular powers. Those precepts
lead of their own accord to equality before the law, to religious
toleration and to popular sovereignty. But they also embody a
distinctive vision of the human being as a free and accountable
individual, answerable for his faults but duty-bound to respect
the freedom and otherness of his neighbour.

That vision is rooted in the sense of nationhood. It is the
basis of responsible citizenship. It has been incorporated into
the legal systems of Europe, both the Roman law traditions that
have prevailed on the continent and the common law traditions
of England and Ireland. Both systems employ in common the
concept of the responsible person, to describe the individual
human being as accountable for his life and actions. The same
vision of the responsible individual has inspired European
art and literature ever since, and it underlies the distinctive

achievements of European civilization in the fields of science and politics. But the focus of this vision is not *Europe* at all. The idea of Europe, as a physical or political entity, features nowhere in the context of what we term a 'Western' civilization in its post-Enlightenment phase. We are right to treasure this identity, which unites us with some of the greatest human achievements, and which puts at our disposal the means of communication with the entire human world. It is an identity that we share with the North Americans, the Australians and the South Americans, that is constantly absorbing into itself the cultural and intellectual expressions of other ways of life. And it is an identity that incorporates those universal practices, such as natural science, civil law and tonal music, which speak to human nature everywhere.

Such an identity, at such depth, cannot be reproduced by artifice, at the rate that the EU is currently being constructed. It took three-and-a-half centuries of civilization after the Peace of Westphalia to embed a distinct national identity that is felt, to a greater or lesser degree, by people born and bred throughout Europe. This sense of oneness is shaping the linguistic, geographical and cultural boundaries of Europe and is shaped by it. Nobody wakes in the morning with the instinctive certainty that she is European, in the way that she is French, German, Scottish or Czech. Not many of us would risk our lives to defend Europe, or willingly pay our taxes to any government other than the one that we identify, through our national loyalty, as *ours*. This sense of national identity is visceral in the literal sense: gut-felt. That of European identity is more exalted, more a matter of brain than heart, more aspirational and also, for that very reason, more elusive and fragile. The identity bestowed by territory and self-government is rooted and self-evident; that nourished by European historical, ethical and cultural ties is something that we must think about in order to embrace.

This exalted and fragile European identity is precious. It needs gentle and careful nurturing if it is to grow into something of political value. This is why I am so deeply concerned about the ongoing effort to fabricate a European identity by symbols of statehood, deliberate persuasion and an avalanche of regulations, in the hope that it will somehow provide for the EU the kind of underpinning that an intuitive national sentiment provides to our national laws.

The risk to a nascent sense of European identity is further aggravated by the dangerous illusion that is conveyed in the official European documents, which urge us to attach ourselves to our European identity, while emptying that identity of its spiritual and historical content. For this sense of identity rests not only on the foundation of a purely rational Enlightenment; it is rooted in the Jewish bible and in the Christian vision of the soul. It is not an identity that is easily shared by Muslims, whose religion, in its more vehement forms, refuses to admit the legitimacy of secular government or the equality of all subjects without regard to sex or creed. Nor is it an identity shared by Christian communities that have not experienced the evolution that shaped the nation states of Europe. It is an identity that involves a particular form of pre-political loyalty, a particular form of attachment between neighbours, of the kind that makes freedom under law into a real possibility. And this loyalty is the kind of loyalty that supports and is supported by the nation state. The fact is that we have *won through* to our identity: that it is attached to the continent of Europe only because it is there that the struggles and achievements occurred.

This venture into the problematic domain of identity is not an entirely academic exercise. The question of Turkey's accession throws a sharp light (or perhaps a shadow) on our deliberations. The rejection of a Muslim Turkey would be a defining 'no' to the meaning of European identity. For the setting of definite

boundaries would establish frontiers of culture, religion and
civilization, clearly defining who we are and who are the Others.
On the other hand, shutting out a country like Turkey would be
to the detriment of fundamental European values. According to
Lydia, the European Union is a Kantian project promoting per-
petual peace through democratic inclusion. By integrating Turkey, Europe could prove both to itself and to the outside world
that it is a truly 'open society' in the sense of Karl Popper's
model of a distinct civilization. Truth to tell, Lydia and I are at
one in not knowing how to resolve this dilemma, at least not
within the strictures of the current EU construct. The European
identity is precious to us both but we differ in our approach.

I believe that, if we are to be true to our European identity, this cannot be by turning our backs on the nation state.
For nationality is Europe's great achievement, and it is on the
experience of nationality that the new Europe should be constructed: a Europe of sovereign nation states in which powers conferred on the central institutions can be freely regained
from them, just as soon as they are abused. If we are not careful,
a centralized and unaccountable bureaucracy, trying to build an
artificial identity by piling law upon law and regulation upon
regulation, will only alienate the people. The institutions of the
EU, on present form, are more calculated to destroy that identity than to protect it. If we do not do something about it, the
greatest enemy of a European identity may well turn out to be
the politicized European Union itself.

Nationhood, Citizenship and Accountability

My friend Lydia sees the European project as an off-spring of the Enlightenment: the calm translation into law of universal values. Its purpose has been to break down old and exclusive loyalties and to replace them with a trans-national idea of citizenship. She regrets over-regulation; but, for her, regulations are needed to re-fashion our mutual dealings according to a legal paradigm: 'When law governs the relations between people it is not war but litigation that resolves their conflicts; and when conflicts are resolved by law they create lasting precedents that guide people's future conduct and ensure that henceforth peace is the norm,' she says. 'This is the promise of Europe, and it is distressing that old national rivalries have invaded the legislative process and perverted it from its goal. What we need is a truly European patriotism – the legislative institutions of Europe should continue to create a trans-national identity that replaces the loyalties fostered by the nation states.'

I respect Lydia's Enlightenment vision, and I too hope for a world of free citizens in which the destructive chauvinisms of the past are kept as far as possible out of politics. But I cannot help

feeling that citizenship, while it is indeed a gift of the Enlightenment, is also impossible without the nation state. A society of
citizens is a society in which strangers can trust one another,
since everyone is bound by a common set of rules. This does not
mean that there are no thieves or swindlers; it means that trust
can grow between strangers, and does not depend upon family connections, tribal loyalties or favours granted and earned.
The existence of this kind of trust in a society of strangers is a
rare achievement, whose pre-conditions are not easily fulfilled.
However, citizenship means living with strangers on terms that
may be, in the short-term, disadvantageous. It means being
prepared to fight battles and suffer losses on behalf of people
whom one neither knows nor wants to know. It means appro-
priating the policies that are made in one's name and endorsing
them as 'ours', even when one disagrees with them. Only when
people have a strong sense of who 'we' are, why 'we' are acting
in this way or that, will they be sufficiently involved in the collective decisions to adopt them as their own. This first-person
plural is the precondition of democratic politics, and must be
safeguarded at all costs, since the price of losing it is social disintegration. It is what we mean, or ought to mean, by nationhood. Those who wish to replace the first-person plural of the
nation ought to be clear what they wish to put in its place.
What other form of membership is supposed to replace that of
the nation and provide the kind of support that national loyalty
has provided for territorial jurisdiction and a secular rule of
law? Nations are composed of neighbours, in other words of
people who share a territory. Hence, they stand in need of a
territorial jurisdiction. Territorial jurisdictions require legislation, and therefore a political process. This process transforms
shared territory into a shared identity. And that identity is the
nation state. There you have a brief summary of American history: people settling together, solving their conflicts by law,

making that law for themselves, and in the course of this process defining themselves as a 'we', whose shared assets are the land and its law.

Now, people cannot share territory without sharing many other things too: language, customs, markets and (in European conditions) a spiritual and religious inheritance. Hence, every territorial jurisdiction will be associated with complex and interlocking loyalties to beliefs, cultures and dynasties. The law treats individuals as bearers of rights and duties. It recasts their relations with their neighbours in abstract terms; it shows a preference for contract over status and for definable interests over inarticulate bonds. It is hostile to all power and authority that is not exerted from within the jurisdiction. In short, it imprints on the community a distinctive political form.

At the same time, we must not think of territorial jurisdiction as merely a conventional arrangement: a kind of ongoing and severable agreement, of the kind that appealed to the Social Contract thinkers of the Enlightenment. It involves a genuine 'we' of membership: not as visceral as that of kinship; not as uplifting as that of worship, but for those very reasons more suited to the modern world and to a society of strangers in which faith is dwindling or dead. To put the matter simply: nations are defined not by kinship or religion but by a homeland. Europe owes its greatness to the fact that the primary loyalties of the European people have been detached from religion and re-attached to the land. Those who believe that the division of Europe into nations has been the primary cause of European wars should remember the devastating wars of religion that national loyalties finally brought to an end. And they should study our art and literature, which is an art and literature not of war but of peace, an invocation of home and the routines of home, of gentleness, everydayness and enduring settlement. Its quarrels are domestic quarrels, its protests are pleas for neighbours, its goal is homecoming and contentment with the place that is ours. That is what we have been taught by Balzac, Proust and Péguy, by Manzoni, Calvino and Lampedusa, by Hölderlin, Kleist and Thomas Mann, by Němcová and Mickiewicz, by Austen, Arnold and T.S. Eliot.

When I rehearsed this argument in front of Lydia I was impressed by the vehement headshaking with which she received it. Finally, unable to contain herself, she burst out that I was confusing two very different things, the patriotism on which we all depend in emergencies, and the nationalism, which has so often been the cause of them. 'What you are describing', she said, 'is not the political sphere, but the social sphere that is governed by it. I have no difficulty in accepting this "first-person plural" to which you refer, this society of strangers bound in the reciprocal tie of citizenship. It is what Hegel meant by civil society, when he drew his famous distinction between civil society and state. But, like Hegel, you imagine that the state must be formed from the same raw material of loyalty, obedience and goodwill that binds neighbour to neighbour in a small community, or member to member in the nuclear family. You imagine that the state and the nation must coincide. That is the dangerous doctrine that led to Bismarck's belligerence, and to the 20th-century wars. And it is in order to point the way to another, more genial and more distant relation between state and civil society that the European Union exists. We can enjoy all our local loyalties in peace time, and call upon them in our great emergencies, without making them hostage to the nation state. It suffices to acknowledge our shared interest, as Europeans, in an over-arching rule of law.'

I have often heard that argument, although seldom so succinctly expressed. And it seems to me to neglect the very need for loyalty which it purports to emphasize. Loyalty cannot be merely a local matter. It must coincide with the reach of citizenship and acknowledge the same boundaries as the law. Only in that way will it enable people to make the sacrifices required by a society of strangers, in which people lead different lives and follow different gods. The first-person plural of nationhood, unlike those of tribe or religion, is intrinsically tolerant of difference. It involves a discipline of neighbourliness, a respect for privacy, and a desire for citizenship, in which people maintain sovereignty over their own lives and the kind of distance that makes such sovereignty possible. Lydia's words notwithstanding, we should distinguish clearly nationalism from national loyalty.

When the Abbé Sieyès declared the aims of the French Revolution, it was in the language of nationalism: 'The nation is prior to everything. It is the source of everything. Its will is always legal. The manner in which a nation exercises its will does not matter; the point is that it does exercise it; any procedure is adequate, and its will is always the supreme law.' Those words express the very opposite of a true national loyalty. Not only do they involve an idolatrous deification of the 'Nation', elevating it far above the people of whom it is in fact composed. They do so in order to punish, to exclude, to threaten rather than to facilitate citizenship and to guarantee peace. And it prepared the way for that massive seizure and concentration of power in a central political machine that has ever since been the principal threat to the security of Europe.

Nationalism is a belligerent *ideology*. In every case, we should distinguish its inflammatory, quasi-religious call to recreate the world from national loyalty of the kind that is expressed even now in the contests between nations in Europe. Nationalism belongs to those surges of religious emotion that have so often led to European war. National loyalty is the explanation of that more durable, less noticeable and less interesting thing, which is European peace.

Lydia did not question any of this. In fact, she thought no-one would disagree with my, rather elementary, exposition of the basics of nationhood. But she pointed out that I was talking about the past not the future. Whilst acknowledging that nation states are the building blocks of the European Union because they are ultimately the only means of implementing the Union's laws, supplying its funds and delivering its content, this is just a transitional stage. According to her, the nation states are not eternal. They are a product of history, with many of them, like Germany and Italy or many of the New Member States, of relatively recent origin. There are significant trends, globalization being one of them, which will, sooner or later, lead to their demise. The Union itself will inevitably accelerate this process.

Lydia continued, 'European citizenship has been enshrined in the treaties and the European *demos* is being created as we speak. One is not born a European, one becomes one. Even if the intensities of national sentiment vary from country to country, they will all fade in the measure that the political union is successful. It is precisely this new nationhood we should strive to build. It is where we should invest our future. If the people were given the chance, enlightened by the great ideals of the project under construction, they would opt for a democratic, federal Europe. It is the outdated, vestigial attachment to nations that stands as a screen between the citizens and their rightful European inheritance.'

Whether the nation state is in terminal decline, and if so what novel political organism takes its place, is but conjecture. In the meantime, we are faced with the real issue of how best to guarantee accountability of political life. This leads us to the topic of citizenship and its connection to nationhood.

Citizenship is not a modern idea. In the celebrated funeral speech, which Thucydides attributed to Pericles, the idea of the free citizen is put forward with exemplary clarity. Pericles encouraged his audience to believe that it was to preserve the benefits of citizenship that the Athenian dead had perished. The Athenian citizen, in Pericles's idealized understanding, was free and tolerant in his private life, in public obedient to the law. He was subject to no-one, and the law that governed him was a law that he accepted uncomplainingly, knowing that it resulted from the free association among citizens, in the assembly where they could debate their common good. The *civis romanus* was likewise a privileged being in the world of the Roman Empire, tied to the Emperor not as subject to sovereign, but as a free partner to a mutual contract. With the Renaissance, the ancient idea of citizenship was revived, soon to become a promise offered to everyone, as the philosophers of the Enlightenment developed theories of political order based on the freedom, equality and sovereignty of the human person. Contentious though their arguments may be, the ideas of those philosophers have entered the pool of received wisdom in the West, finding embodiment first in the American Constitution and subsequently in the efforts throughout Europe both to extend the franchise and to offer a contract of citizenship to everyone.

The offer of citizenship should not be seen as a mere by-product of 19th-century politics. It emerged from the concerted attempt, involving all strands of society and all shades of opinion, to accommodate the industrial revolution and the social and geographical mobility that came with it. It invited people to see themselves as bound in a web of contractual obligations, each protected in his sovereign sphere, and each enjoying rights against others and against the state. Modern citizenship is not, of course, the same in every respect as ancient citizenship: it is a relationship arising in a 'great society', as Adam Smith described it, a society of strangers governed by a law-making and law-abiding state. Modern citizenship is the relation between the state and the individual in which each is fully accountable to the other. It consists in a web of reciprocal rights and duties, upheld by a rule of law that stands higher than either party. Although the state enforces the law, it enforces it equally against itself and against the private citizen. The citizen has rights which the state is duty-bound to uphold, and also duties which the state has a right to enforce. Because these rights and duties are defined and limited by the law, citizens have a clear conception of where their freedoms end.

The rise of modern citizenship is simultaneous with the rise of the nation state, for the simple reason that they are one and the same. The condition of citizenship would be impossible without a state to which the citizen's duty is owed and on which his rights and privileges depend. People can live their citizenship only in conditions receptive to local and national loyalties. Any attempt to override the nation state, or cancel its fundamental claim to the allegiance of its members, will threaten the foundations of citizenship. This is what we see happening as the trans-national European regime of regulation steadily erodes and marginalizes the legal inheritance and sovereignty of the European nations. Already in several countries of the EU, notably Spain, Belgium, Italy, the UK and the Balkans, the promotion of an overarching EU identity reinforces internal disintegration. There is growing power in the state periphery, leading to multi-level blurred identities of a medieval sort. Today, this is aggravated by the arrival of growing numbers of EU or non-EU immigrants. The weaker the state, the easier it becomes for Brussels to impose itself, or for other, more affirmed nation states to take over power at the EU level.

To put it bluntly, every aspect of the European decision-making process lacks precisely the kind of accountability that is the norm in the well-established parliamentary democracies. The European institutions have been set up with peremptory speed and without regard to the conditions which might generate their popular acceptance. An obvious instance is provided by the Commission itself. It is to be hoped that the most blatant corruption scandals might be a thing of the past. However, no accountant has been able to pass unqualified accounts for the Commission for the last 12 years, an untenable situation for any other public or private entity. Vast sums of money from the EU budget, funds and subsidies disbursed to the Member States still have a tendency to disappear. Investigations of OLAF, a quasi-independent EU body to fight financial fraud, have revealed continuing corruption at Commission, European Parliament and member state level. Its own chief currently faces allegations of conflicts of interest and irregularities in the way it operates. Yet there is no sequel, apart from the censure of the accountant, or the persecution and dismissal of those 'whistle-blowers' who have dared to report on the Commission outside its fortified walls.

Accountability is a rare achievement, made possible in Europe by the rise of the nation state, and remaining intimately connected to the national political process. European institutions that by-pass national loyalty or over-ride the representative institutions, through which the people of Europe have secured control over their leadership, will simply destroy the only forms of accountability that we Europeans know.

Lydia's response was nothing if not trenchant: 'The power struggle between those who are grimly hanging on to a national past and its fading institutions and those who are intent on creating a viable European political entity will continue to define the coming decades. But, in the end, only federalism at European level could provide the answer to the missing sense of belonging and to what is currently perceived as the so-called democratic deficit. Democracy is always messy. The current EU merely mirrors the situation in most Member States where a consensus has always had the upper hand over continuous,

detailed consultation with the general population. In the mainstream of European tradition, political decisions have mostly
been taken by an inner circle of governing parties which managed to secure parliamentary majority. People, on the whole,
are content to vote from time to time and do not constantly
question the legitimacy of those who rule them.'

In Lydia's opinion, 'we actually have a democratic *surplus*
instead of a deficit. You can measure a democratic deficit by
people rioting in the streets calling for more democracy. This
has not happened. In a sense, the Union might be suffering
from the plight and blight of all politics in Europe, namely a
crisis of liberal democracy in modern societies. But there is
at least as much transparency in the European process as is in
the governments of most nation states. In some cases, European institutions easily surpass national ones. The full text of
inter-governmental conferences is published, the Commission
invites open consultation and debate on legislative projects *via*
Green and White papers, the drafting of legislation is done in
cooperation with delegates of the Member States and under co-
decision also with the European Parliament, while the final text
is available to every interested European citizen well before the
various parliaments determine the exact form of its transposi-
tion. If the system appears undemocratic, it is precisely because
not all national parliaments are doing their scrutinizing jobs
in the first place! Every document sent to the Council by the
Commission is also sent to national parliaments, with Commissioners attending national parliamentary hearings. The deficit,
if it is a deficit, belongs to the nation state and not to the Union.
The diffusion of responsibility in the current system is in the
interest of national actors: successes are claimed by the countries themselves and mishaps conveniently blamed on the EU.

Up until now, we have only had two varieties of democracies – the Greek city state and the nation state. The Euro-

pean Union is a third level. It is no less than the reinvention of democracy as a post-national institution. I admit that we might not have discovered adequate tools for decision-making yet. But the alternative you seem to be advocating, which is more inter-governmentalism, cannot be the answer.

The problem, Publia, is that you have assumed accountability to be always downwards, from those with power to those beneath them. But it can go the other way, as in an army. True accountability is a three-term relationship, as when an army officer is held accountable to his superior for the men under his command. The Brussels machine, as you call it, is accountable in just that way, not *to* the citizens of Europe, but *for* them. And it accounts to the Council of Ministers who are themselves ultimately answerable to their national parliaments and, through those parliaments, to the people who elected them. This seems to me like an excellent chain of responsibility. We should not discard it; rather we should strengthen the links.'

'I profoundly disagree,' I retorted. 'While attack may be the best form of defence, it is a risky manoeuvre; here it has not served you well. The so-called "democratic deficit" in the European institutions is a built-in feature. The institutions were set up in such a way that they could be influenced from below, but controlled only from above. Accountability, however, means just the reverse: influence from above, but control from below – control by those whose interest is served, and who retain the ultimate remedy of dismissal from office. True subsidiarity means that those who surrender their powers to some higher court or parliament retain the ability to eject its officers for abuse of those powers.

This ability is presupposed in the modern idea of citizenship, which views the powers of government as conferred by the consent of the citizens, a consent which can be withdrawn at an election. This kind of control from below (which is what we mean, or ought to mean, by democracy) is not easily achieved. It was achieved in Europe only at the end of a long and painful process of nation-building. The nation state offered to its members a common loyalty, a way of envisaging their togetherness, which made the project of electing and ejecting their representatives intelligible to the ordinary citizen. They were able to acquire that strange habit – unknown in most of the world – of regarding people, whom they intensely disliked and would never vote for, as nevertheless entitled to govern them. Bound together by ties of nationhood, and trusting the political process that gave ultimate control to the citizens, the members of nation states have been able to create institutions which hold their leaders and representatives to account for everything that affects the common interest.'

Lydia's notion of democratic surplus is charming, but no more than that. It fails to answer the old question – *Quis custodiet ipsos custodes?* The alternative to Lydia's vision is a Europe of nation states that retain control over all matters that touch their national interests, and which surrender their powers either reversibly or not at all. In other words, a Europe that is accountable to the people.

The Single Market

Lydia and I are equally well informed as to the origins of the Single Market. Its history is not a matter of contention between us. It was entirely natural that the founders of the European project should believe that free trade would be the basis of trust and friendship between the European nations. This belief was also reinforced by recent memories of the Depression, which had been intensified by the universal retreat into protectionist policies. The fashioning of a new world order of reconciliation and the rebuilding of Europe, therefore, clearly demanded a reversion to the older regime of economic freedom.

However, this freedom was, from the beginning, understood in a highly qualified way. The decision was taken to create a 'common market' that would be compatible on the one hand with German federalism and on the other with the centralized and *dirigiste* economy that had grown in France. At the time, the German political elite, led by Konrad Adenauer and his finance minister Ludwig Erhard, was heavily influenced by Austrian economics, and in particular by the 'social market' philosophy of Wilhelm Röpke. The aim of this philosophy was to reconcile the free economy defended by von Mises and Hayek with the social needs and moral autonomy of the 'little platoon'. The hope was to build a free economy without sacrificing local communities and the loyalties on which they depended, while at the same time opening Germany to the benefits of international trade.

The French political class had no corresponding commitment to free markets. Large sections of industry were nationalized, and all forms of economic activity looked to the state for subsidies and protection. The Communist Party and its powerful allies in the large trade unions were actively campaigning against free enterprise, and left-wing coalition governments acquiesced in the traditional state domination of the economy. In such a context, the concept of free trade takes on a new meaning. How can a country encourage free competition from abroad, when it can barely tolerate free competition within its borders? The Treaty of Rome, therefore, embodied an historic Franco-German compromise. The Single Market, as it is now known, was designed to open the lines of trade between the Member States, while keeping in place a regime of intervention and subsidies through which the economy of France was managed by the state. The arrangement promised internal free trade and unified external tariffs – in other words, a customs union. In all matters to do with trade, both with each other, and with the rest of the world, the Member States surrendered their independence, and undertook to be guided by a single, and developing, set of regulations. Some of my British friends regret this so deeply, and are such ardent advocates of open competition in the new global economy, that they would like to reverse history and reinstate the rival concept – advanced at the time by Erhard and Adenauer – of a free trade area, in which the nation states retain their sovereignty in matters to do with external trade. However, that is not how the Treaties

have been formulated, and any attempt to restore the right of
Member States to negotiate their own external trade treaties
will be tantamount to a withdrawal from the Union, which I
don't advocate.

Nor are we, two friends, divided on the inherent tensions
generated by Treaties that embody such an uneasy compromise, advancing economic freedom while also impeding it.
This illustrates a recurring difficulty with the 'Single Market'
idea, which requires Member States to remove internal barriers, even though they thereby expose favoured assets to the
risk of external competition or control. The difficulties are
well exemplified by the Common Agricultural Policy (CAP),
designed to protect the French rural economy from the large-
scale producers of the Commonwealth and the Americas. This
policy was insisted upon by the French as the price of opening
French markets to German industrial goods.

Initially, the CAP had two purposes: to make Europe self-
sufficient in food, and to support the small farmer, whose status as a symbol of European peace, stability and beneficence
had been the constant theme of war-time propaganda. Self-
sufficiency was achieved, largely on account of worldwide
improvements in the methods of farming; but the first victim of
this was the peasant farmer. Farm subsidies push up the price,
and therefore the rental value, of land, so penalizing the small
producer who rents his fields, whilst favouring large landown-
ers and agribusiness. Hence, while the EU makes payments to
over 100,000 different farms and agribusinesses, the top 100
recipients receive over 23% of the total, while the bottom 50%
take only 2.6% – which means that the policy is entirely ineffective in directing support to the small farmer. Furthermore,
the CAP has maintained food prices at an artificially high level
throughout Europe, costing the average family an extra 1500
euro a year. It has also produced surpluses, which it has dumped

on international markets, further alienating food-producing countries elsewhere; and it has destroyed local food economies across the continent by imposing finicky standards with which only the supermarket chains and the agribusinesses can easily comply. The point is not to carp on the failings of CAP. These are well attested and reforms of it are ongoing. It is to highlight the fundamental differences of approach between countries like France and the USA, intent on protecting their indigenous agriculture, and countries like Britain and Sweden, whose priority is the provision of cheap food from all over the world. The question is how to fit such diametrically opposed approaches into one over-arching economic framework.

The original Treaty of Rome presented 'four freedoms' as integral to the new 'common market': free movement of goods, free movement of services, free movement of capital and free movement of labour. The last two freedoms form no part of a 'customs union' as this had previously been conceived, nor, indeed, is the free movement of services thought to be necessary to the abolition of tariffs. And all three of the new freedoms of movement – services, labour and capital – have come to pose unexpected or conveniently ignored difficulties.

Now there is no doubt that the movement of labour has benefits as well as costs, and that, properly managed, it could contribute greatly to the prosperity and solidarity of the European peoples. At the time of the Treaty of Rome, the original signatories enjoyed comparable standards of living. The movement of workers between them would, it was plausibly assumed, be minimal, and in any case in no single direction. Expansion of the Union, however, has opened the door to massive one-way migrations, from countries ruined by communism to others in which opportunities and benefits are freely available. This is a situation that calls out for management. In the opinion of the ordinary citizen, confronted with a large-scale influx of people in competition for his livelihood, the government must do something to restrict the flow. That is what governments are for. But it is only *national* governments that can do anything about it. And that is precisely what they do. The French and the Germans have put up barriers to limit the flow of Polish workers. The British, belatedly, did the same to try to stem the flow of Romanians and Bulgarians. When it comes to the crunch, nation states eventually put their own vital interests first in defiance of the Union rules and the Union can do precious little about it.

The classical economists acknowledged that migration of labour to the place where it can be most profitably employed is a natural part of the free economy. They were also aware of the social disruption that could ensue when new industries in the towns drew workers from the fields. However, they believed that, in the long run, when friction had worn away, new forms of solidarity would replace the old. As we know from the history of the 19th century, these new forms of solidarity were a long time in the making. They depended upon constant appeals, at all levels of society, to sentiments of nationhood and shared destiny; they transcribed themselves into laws which, from the English Factory Acts to Bismarck's *Sozialgesetzgebung* of 1884–9, were express constraints on the free market; and they addressed the new class of socially mobile workers with promises of political participation and active citizenship of a kind that had been the historical privilege of aristocracies. Enormous efforts were expended, by legislators, churches, charities and public-spirited people, by philosophers, novelists and social reformers, and by the people themselves, in understanding and coming to terms with the new situation. And, if their efforts were rewarded with success, this should not be seen as an inevitable result of a free economy, but rather as proof of the moral and spiritual capital that had been invested in the nation state.

The Treaty of Rome has deprived people of one of the most important safeguards of their social assets – namely, a government prepared to secure national borders against incoming migration. The 'four freedoms' were imposed from above on people who were given no effective say in the matter, and who were deprived of the one instrument – national sovereignty – through which they could defend their interests. National sovereignty involves the right to determine who resides within the national borders, who controls the nation's assets and who is entitled to the advantages of citizenship. It presupposes a 'we' from which our bargaining begins and whose interests that bargaining serves. By incorporating into the Treaty of Rome provisions calculated to weaken national sovereignty, the founders of the European project ensured that the project would be increasingly perceived as a battle-ground for competing national interests, as Member States fight to retain control of social and economic assets that might otherwise be confiscated by the Union.

Nor has the free movement of capital been any less problematic. The facility of relocating residences and enterprises across national boundaries is again one that can bring substantial benefits. As with the movement of labour, however, there is a growing resistance to national assets, or what are considered such, being acquired by foreign entities. Increasingly, therefore, the Member States are flouting EU rules. The French government, for example, ring-fenced large sectors of the economy, entitled 'of strategic interest', which are forbidden to any foreign acquisition, including by EU members. The merger between the French utility Suez and Gaz de France was facilitated in order to create a 'national champion', being just one of the ways through which a member state can circumvent the intention of the single market. The hostility of certain Member States to 'foreign ownership' is, however, understandable. It is a reminder that the movement of capital, like the movement of people, although promised under the Treaty of Rome as a 'freedom', is a movement that should always be managed, not only in the interests of free enterprise, but also in the interests of national sovereignty.

The matters that I have touched on remind us of an important principle, which is that markets are self-regulating devices only to the extent that they safeguard the autonomy of their participants. And this autonomy is exercised not only at the economic level, but also at the social level, through the free association among neighbours and through the development of institutions, networks and clubs. It is also manifest at the political level, through participatory democracy. Such is the 'social market' ideal supposedly adopted by the Treaty of Rome. Treaties between sovereign states need not involve a loss of autonomy, any more than a contract between individuals involves a loss of freedom. On the contrary, contract and treaty are both expressions of sovereignty, and the axiom that *pacta sunt servanda* is, like Kant's categorical imperative, a law expressing the freedom of those who are bound by it. The Treaty of Rome could, if interpreted in the spirit in which it was originally signed, still function as a willed expression of the sovereignty of its signatories. As now interpreted, however, the Treaty goes beyond any conventional interpretation of how treaties operate, and has become an irreversible surrender, more akin to a marriage vow than a contract. And this is where Lydia and I start to part company. She has an altogether different perspective. I hope my summary of our many conversations does her justice:

'A common economic space as the heart of European integration has produced enormous economic and social benefits far outweighing potential and actual negative externalities. There is a direct correlation between market size and the strength of the enterprises and economies it contains. Firms greatly benefit from operating in a common regulatory space, while individuals not only reap a greater variety of cheaper high quality goods and services, but also dramatically increase their chances for economic success. With the Single Market, we have managed a tremendous feat: to foster economic growth without destroying the instruments of social protection and redistribution of wealth, thus reconciling the principle of competition with the noble heritage of the European welfare state.'

'History', said Lydia, 'is about ideas inspiring people. As Victor Hugo once said, "an idea whose time has come unleashes an insurmountable force". You could indeed say that European economic integration has been the brainchild of a European elite dreaming of European reconciliation and unity as a way of reconstructing an economically and morally broken continent. However, those leading minds did not advance in a vacuum. They based their actions on a consensus among their fellow Europeans, which had tasted for the umpteenth time the bitter consequences of nationalism run amok. Far from being undemocratic, the structures organically emerging have enshrined the popular will of the peoples of Europe to give their destinies a new shape.

Diversity is one of our undeniable strengths! The national characteristics so dear to both our hearts have their rightful place in Europe. They are even specifically nurtured under European law through the various protection of origin schemes. Let us not forget that, in the name of sovereignty and historical traditions, citizens have often been forced to accept mediocre goods and services by their governments. The break-up of national monopolies would never have happened without the prodding of the European Commission (EC), a force that has consistently acted to safeguard and enhance competition.

Far from being inflexible, the Single Market has shown tremendous capacity for change. Its initial emphasis on agri-

cultural subsidies to sweeten the seemingly bitter pill of competition is largely on its way out. European financial support is
now devoted to encouraging small-scale farming and rural sustainable development, actively preventing individual countries
from coddling their agricultural lobbies.

The Single Market is a regulatory edifice that needs to be
seen as a whole. All elements, both the rules and compliance with
them, need to be in place for it to work smoothly. While regulating the internal market should be left to the European level,
administration and implementation belong as close to the citizen
as possible. This is what I would call subsidiarity in action.

Admittedly, some deficiencies remain, especially in the
uneven application of Single Market rules and regulations. For
example, I deeply regret the clumsy curtailing of the freedom
of labour after enlargement took place. It suffices to look at the
three economies that did not impose any such bans to see that
adhering to the four freedoms is not only fair, but enormously
beneficial from an economic point of view. I am also shocked as
to how liberalization of services has been seized upon by dema-
gogues who cloud the minds of ordinary people with skewed
arguments. Look at the economic improvements experienced
by many countries, especially the smaller countries, largely
thanks to the Single Market. Mobility is a major driver of internal reform, as, in the long term, countries will adapt in order to
attract the most skilled professionals. Finally, let me conclude
here with a counter factual assessment. What would have happened without the European project? There would surely be
less of a single market in Europe, hence less economic growth,
probably even worse agricultural protectionism, more dispar-
ity in the legal frameworks of European countries and more
subsidization of non-competitive industry.'

Lydia sipped her coffee and looked at me enquiringly. I grant
that a common market requires some degree of harmonization

of standards, as well as the abolition of subsidies, tariffs, monopolies and unfair procedures, and to this extent the introduction of far-reaching regulation was inevitable. No-one would wish to deny the many great successes that can be attributed to the European process, in the break-up of cartels, in the opening up of European markets and, not least, in facilitating the transition from communist to free-market economies. But the fundamental tensions and consequent difficulties will not diminish. They are certain to aggravate conditions in the European economy because the attempt to resolve all such difficulties involves simply more laws and regulations. In fact, the process of regulation has recognized no *a priori* limits. Since almost any aspect of human society has an impact, however indirect, on the way in which goods are produced, consumed and exchanged, the pursuit of a 'single market' can be used to legislate for or against virtually anything.

We should also bear in mind that regulations can be used as effectively to destroy competition as to promote it. A country whose economy has been crippled by laws regarding the hours and conditions of work can export the cost of those laws by imposing them on its competitors. Or a country can lobby for regulations which favour native financial institutions over their foreign rivals. These things, as we know, are happening continually in the EU process, to the extent that it is no longer at all clear whether trade between the nation states of Europe has been furthered or hampered by the regulatory regime. All that is certain is that the economic life of Europe is increasingly controlled from the centre. We cannot, in my view, reconcile the diverse interests and economic cultures of our continent by regulation alone. We have to accept that national interests will remain the predominant forces that shape European politics. When nations agree to eliminate barriers to reciprocal trade they surrender only powers affecting tariffs, mergers, monopo-

lies, certain aspects of competition and such like but safeguard
their own laws regarding working hours, employment rights,
consumer protection and a host of matters, the details of which
form the matrices of who we are. Such a distinction is perfectly
compatible with the existence of Europe-wide treaties of free
trade and a European Court of Justice empowered to adjudi-
cate disputes between contracting parties.

I doubt that Lydia was persuaded by all of my arguments.
Our conversation then veered to the relationship of Europe with
the rest of the world. We had been to the same university, so we
both knew the theory: classical economists attacked protectionism largely because it discouraged countries from making use
of their most important assets, which are the labour, capital and
ingenuity of their citizens. Prosperity comes with international
competition and specialization. The successful search for markets enables each nation to exhibit and profit from its human
capital. It was from an instinctive awareness of that truth that
the GATT was set up in 1947, with the purpose of eliminating
discrimination and reducing barriers to trade. Its successor, the
WTO, has continued its remarkably successful policies, which
have all but eliminated the high tariff walls that had produced
so much instability and hostility during the inter-war years. But
globalization and unrestrained information flow, in their manifold ramifications, create a host of formidable challenges for
everyone. How does, how should, Europe react?

When the Single Market was first being created there were
many in the EC who saw it less as an exercise in free trade
than as a barrier against it – a way to create 'fortress Europe'.
This defensive frame of mind was understandable, given the
social and economic fragility of the nations that had lost almost
everything in their struggle to survive the war. At the time, it
was possible to think that this protectionism would be a temporary measure, allowing the European economies to stabilize

under the benign effect of mutual commerce. But, of course, the instinct to defend what we own, in both national and continental sphere, is too deep rooted to be tamed out of existence. As a Trade Commissioner put it at the beginning of the 1990s: 'We are not building a single market in order to turn it over to hungry foreigners.'

It is important to recognize that the EU has a declining share of the world economy, and intra-EU trade relative to total EU trade has been declining in relative terms since its peak in 1992. The main opportunities for trade expansion lie in other markets: India, China, the rest of Asia and the USA. Unless Europe opens its trade to these areas it will gradually become insignificant as a world economic force: already reputable forecasters, including the EC itself, anticipate a drop in the EU share in world GDP by 50% or more by 2050. With the growth of long-term unemployment on the continent, the looming crisis in pension provision and loss of competitiveness, protectionism becomes less defensible even as it becomes more seductive. The Commission, under its current leadership, is fully converted to market liberalization but lacks the power to overcome resistance from those Member States that have an instinctive aversion to the realities of global trade.

Naturally, Lydia dissents. She sees the 27 member countries never being able to compete on their own with the US and Japan, let alone China and India. How could Latvia or Hungary negotiate successfully a separate deal with Russia for vital natural resources, or Italy control incredibly cheap consumer product imports from China, or even one of the larger Member States secure more advantageous trading terms with any of the global players than a truly integrated powerful Europe could? For Lydia, Europe faces an enormous challenge: mastering the forces of globalization, harvesting the benefits for its citizens and shielding them from the down side. 'Our overwhelming interest lies therefore in unity, whatever our national differences. Europe cannot be a protectionist bloc. It has to be a responsible actor in an ever faster evolving environment. It has to use its experience in managing globalization in its relations with major powers like China and the US. Europe has an important role to play in shaping globalization – to make sure that social, environmental and consumer protection norms are enshrined by regulatory bodies and ensure that international practice meets the highest standards possible rather than the lowest common denominator. You mustn't fear, Publia, Europe will not be economically irrelevant. There is 14 times more US investment in Holland than there is in all of China. We should turn the attractiveness of our Single Market into an advantage. Instead of passively submitting to globalization, we should formulate robust common strategies for foreign investment by some of our key industries. This is why regulating investments by foreign governments, the so-called Sovereign Funds, is crucial.'

So, how should trade between European nation states and with the outside world be organized? A purist might argue that we should return to the nation states' autonomous powers to deal with their trading partners, since no less is required by the principle of true subsidiarity. However, the resulting oscillation between the powers of nation states and central institutions would produce chaos of uncertainty and would scarcely contribute to free trade or national cohesion. How to reconcile subsidiarity with the genuine achievements of the Single Market is therefore a question that needs deep thought. What kind of legislative regime will reconcile national sovereignty with the free flow of goods and services, labour and capital, while promoting the good neighbourly relations that Europe needs? One that clearly defines the limits for Union action, providing that necessary freedom of action within the delimited area.

As a general principle, by removing barriers we do not merely increase the opportunities for doing business with the rest of the world; we introduce the only real incentive for difficult reform to achieve international competitiveness. Employment, pensions, taxation, monopolies and mergers all will become subject to the much-needed review without which many of the unreformed European economies will decline. Rather than waste away within its fortress, Europe should lower the drawbridge, and step out across the moat. At the same time, the priority of the political leadership of more defensively minded countries is to deepen and accelerate the process of European integration.

So, at the end of the day, Lydia and I concur that one legislative regime may not suffice, at least for the moment, to satisfy the ambitions and needs of the entire continent. The opt-outs may have to be augmented by opt-ins, and the structure of the Union will have to become more flexible if Europe is not to be bogged down by the inherent contradictions of the Single Market as currently set out.

Finance and the Global Economy

The European project was conceived at a time when economic activity was centred on industrial manufacture. The State tended to be strongly involved in the national economy, either in capitalizing industrial ventures that lay beyond the capacity of the private sector or in rescuing key industries from bankruptcy, when needed. Industry was located in places where raw materials and cheap labour were readily available, capitalizing on economies of scale. All this is implied, of course, by the name of what was to be the seedling of the EU: the European Coal and Steel Community (ECSC).

However, the explosive development of communications around the world and the liberation of world trade have produced an entirely new situation. The most vital part of any advanced economy is now the service sector, and the most successful companies are the new 'platform companies', as they have been called, which stick their brand on goods that they would never dream of producing. Firms like IKEA and Toyota are able to expand constantly, while off-loading onto their producers (who are often situated in developing countries) the costs of rapidly changing demand. As the service economy expands, employment or profit suffers less from economic downturns than imports. Any cull in the workforce will occur in places which are without real influence over the domestic politics of the countries where their goods are sold. Meanwhile, the service economy grows, displacing the manufacturing sector from the central place that it occupied, until recently, in all government thinking. Thus, 91% of the American workforce is now employed in the service sector, and even those industries that are engaged in manufacture are beginning to outsource the most volatile parts of their production to countries where organized labour is non-existent.

I have tried to impress upon Lydia that, in times of globalized competition, our principal capital consists of the invisible assets contained in our laws, our financial institutions, our educational traditions and our informal networks of support. Those assets are flexible, adaptable, and contain the accumulated knowledge and experience of many generations. Outside Europe and its diaspora they barely exist. And they would confer on the people of Europe a competitive advantage in the emerging global economy, were we free to use them. Devices like the limited liability company, the purpose trust, the banking system, the stock exchange, the insurance business, even national currencies, did not come into existence by *fiat* from some central power. They emerged gradually over centuries. The innovations of Venetian, Genoan and Florentine merchants and bankers, the institution-building genius of Dutch 17th-century merchants, the clubbable instincts of the City of London financiers, the foresight of Hanseatic traders, not to speak of the Roman law concept of corporate personality and the English law doctrines of contract and trust, all had a part to play in generating the diversified tools of finance and commerce in Europe. Each nation evolved a way of dealing with the complexities of international trade while protecting those who take the risk of it. And in each nation financial, educational and legal institutions became organically connected, and connected to the networks and culture of our cities.

The attempt to impose central control over any part of these delicate structures threatens their most valuable feature: their adaptability. Were the capital assets of Europe vested in infrastructure, engineering works and manufacturing industry, the project of central regulation and control might have seemed sensible in the days of the ECSC. The global economy has moved on since the dreary times of mass production and gargantuan engineering celebrated on Soviet banknotes. The future of Europe depends upon our ability to deploy the asset which endows us with our real competitive edge. This is the social capital embodied in our financial, legal and commercial institutions.

'Whilst it is amusing to offer me implicit association with the USSR, it is also a little mischievous,' Lydia replied. 'Central control can truly liberate. Take the euro, for example. Designed to eliminate currency fluctuation and exchange rate risk, outlaw competitive devaluation and stimulate the economy, the euro has not only been a major economic achievement but also a milestone in the move towards a fully integrated Europe. There was quite a stubborn resistance to abolishing the much-prized Deutsche Mark and one or two other well-established currencies, but the deed is done and cannot be undone. So far, the euro has not led to the expected convergence of the diverse economies and its benefits have not yet fully materialized across the continent. But it is early days. The complaints about inflationary impact of its introduction and the nostalgic longing for the old coins and notes will soon die away whilst some of the beneficial effects are immediate. This is especially evident in the case of smaller countries or countries formerly suffering from currency fluctuations. They are now attracting significant foreign capital because investors have their return secure in the respect-able, stable and low inflation-based currency. Perhaps, ironically, as one of its principal unintended consequences, the introduc-tion of the euro has contributed to the pre-eminence of London – outside the eurozone – as the world premier financial capital (one of the world's three largest financial centres, together with New York and Tokyo) and as the largest financial and business centre in Europe.'

'But your view is contestable on two points, Lydia,' I retorted, 'that of universal benefit and that of irreversibility. Not every country stood to gain from replacing its local cur-rency. It has removed from national governments the power to control interest rates and to revalue or devalue their currency. It does not allow decoupling their economies from those of their neighbours, even when economic circumstances are cry-ing out for such a move. A recent opinion poll suggests that 57% of Germans wish to return to the Mark. According to another poll, a majority of Swedes are now against joining the eurozone. And the Dutch feel badly let down by the change. Remember that they had sacrificed a consistently strong Guil-der. On your assertion that it cannot be undone, I suspect a triumph of hope over evidence.

Look only at the fact that other Member States had opted to stay outside the single currency zone, which the Maastricht Treaty had declared to be 'irrevocable'. In the latest edition of *Mann on the Legal Aspects of Money* (ed. Charles Proctor), which is the bible of international monetary law, a new chapter on with-drawal from the eurozone was added, explaining exactly how it might occur, and what it might mean for financial contracts. Here, as elsewhere, national interest is the ultimate guide to political action; hence, national governments have done their best to regain control over their budgets regardless of the rules supposedly laid down by the adoption of the single currency.

The damage done to the Italian economy is now recognized, with real labour costs in Italy compared to Germany now 40% higher than they were before the launch of the euro. In all cases, traditional ways of managing the economy have been made difficult or impossible. The Growth and Stability Pact of 1997, the cornerstone of establishing the single currency, is dead. The permissible levels of indebtedness have been breached by France and Germany.

It is the position of Italy, however, which shows the real cost of the euro and why it could indeed unravel. The Italian case also shows the danger of making 'irrevocable' decisions concerning matters that no human being, let alone an Italian minister of finance, has ever been able to control. A constantly rising government debt has only been brought to manageable proportions by periodic devaluation. This is no longer an option. Today, Italy's debt stands at 105% of GDP, with interest rates at 4% and GDP growing at 2%, which means that, unless something changes, collapse is unavoidable. And if the only thing that can change is exit from the eurozone, so converting debts in euro into debts in Liras, that is what may well happen. This could have devastating effects throughout the eurozone, not least on the German banks who, trusting in the 'irrevocability' promised in the Maastricht Treaty, have invested in supposedly risk-free Italian bonds. The euro is still an infant, its ultimate fate as yet unknown. Clearly, it benefited some participant states and hindered or endangered others. What is most interesting, and a pointer to the future, is the fact that the roof did not fall in and the Union is functioning just as before with a significant division between the 15 states in the eurozone and 12 currently outside it. Although these numbers may change in the future, the two options could well remain, as many temporary arrangements do, permanent.'

The euro was a political invention, imposed under pressure

from President Mitterrand anxiously responding to the unification of Germany by trying to equalize the two centres of European power. However, it is not political interventions that have
created the economic power of Europe. Rather, it is the legal
devices that have enabled markets to govern themselves outside
the reach of politics. In particular, the genius of Europe has been
manifest in its financial markets, which have enabled European
countries so often to seize the advantage in the world economy.
Even if the bulk of world trade takes place outside Europe, a
disproportionate amount of the needed financial transactions
pass through European institutions, predominantly the City of
London. Through their invisible assets of law, insurance, financ-
ing and accounting, European states have something to offer
the global economy, which is not easily available elsewhere. The
only evident competitors outside the Union are Switzerland
and the United States.

It is entirely typical of the EU, however, that it does not
appreciate the delicacy and organic complexity of this invisible
capital. In its Financial Services Action Plan (FSAP), it proposes a
vast array of new regulations, covering everything from banking,
insurance and investment to the conduct of business and capital
adequacy. The stated purpose – to create a single market in financial services – is not to be confused with the real effect, which
is to create a single regulator for the whole EU market, so curtailing the operating independence of financial organizations in
the Member States. As a form of national protectionism this has
much to commend it, but as a way of deploying one of Europe's
greatest capital assets it is manifestly counterproductive.

Because the FSAP impacts on my own business, I discussed
it with Lydia, who is a client as well as a friend. She had nothing
but good to say of the plan, which she argued to be entirely in
keeping with the original objective of the Treaty of Rome. The
Markets in Financial Instruments Directive, she pointed out,

enables investment firms to conduct business anywhere in the EU; the Market Abuse Directive aims to police markets against fraud, manipulation and insider trading; the Takeovers Directive aims to permit cross-border takeovers, so encouraging the free flow of capital. And so on. Such Directives, honestly and eagerly pursued by the Commissioners appointed to oversee their implementation, are entirely beneficial. They increase competition and the flow of information, especially in places hitherto crippled by socialist dogma and black market dealings. 'In any case,' she went on, 'we should not see the benefits merely in economic terms. The Plan is addressing far deeper problems, concerning the legitimacy of corporate capitalism and the visible face of international finance. We cannot ignore the suspicion with which these things are viewed by the ordinary people of Europe. Nor can we ignore the need to bind the world of finance in moral constraints, and to alert the people of central and eastern Europe that the alternative to communism is not a lawless free-for-all, but a species of honest and accountable dealing. I see the FSAP as part of the moral mission that underlies the European project. I would support it, even if it were shown to be less than efficient when judged in economic terms. To continue deepening the integration and to realize the full potential of the single market in abolishing the barriers in the domain of the service industries in general and the financial services in particular, it is obviously necessary to set standards and introduce detailed regulations across the whole Union.'

Reflecting on Lydia's argument, I concluded that, even if there is a strong moral motive behind the Action Plan, it is a motive that will not be revealed in the resulting Directives, for three reasons. First, the details of the Directives emerge only after intense lobbying from national and sectional interests, so that the final results are remote from any high moral standard. Secondly, the costs involved are burdensome. JP Morgan estimates that compliance with the Markets in Financial Instruments Directive will cost, for eight major European banks, close on 19 billion euro – not counting the loss in revenues that will ensue thereafter. And recent studies suggest that the net result of the legislation, implied or incipient, in the FSAP, will prompt firms established in Europe to settle elsewhere. Instead of raising finance to a higher moral level, the FSAP will simply drive financial services to places where it can find a profitable home. In the third place, and most importantly, finance is the global industry *par excellence*. The success of the City of London is not due to trade within the borders of Great Britain. It is due to the felicitous deployment of human and social capital. The institutions that arose in the City of London made London into the centre of international finance. But those institutions were not created by edicts from the sovereign power. They were the benign by-products of business dealings over generations. Their regulations were created from within, by the need for contracting parties to trust one another. And English law stepped in to make that trust enforceable.

Lydia hastened to reassure me: 'We do all, of course, realize that Britain has a very special interest in this matter, having the City of London as the leading financial centre of Europe and among the top three of the world. No-one questions the vast experience accumulated in its long rise to prominence, nor the consistent rules set by its own Financial Services Authority. But isn't it about time that Europe received part of the praise in this matter? A little while ago, the City of London celebrated 20 years after its 'Big Bang' reforms, which, as you are well aware, hugely increased London's attractiveness as a place to do business, transforming it first into a European and then into a world financial centre. And I don't think anybody mentioned Europe during the festivities, but they certainly should have. The 'Big Bang' happened because the EC Directorate-General for Competition attacked the system of commissions in the City and, concluding that the case would be lost, the regulatory framework in the City was changed. The rest is history. Doesn't anybody in the City of London understand that the EU has been critical to their prosperity and success?

It is not surprising that international institutions like to locate themselves in the City and money from all over the world tends to flow there. Some people say – I am not one of them – that this state of affairs bestows an unfair competitive advantage on London as against Frankfurt, Paris, Milan and other European financial centres. But the primary purpose of the EU regulatory regime is to create a level playing field so that financial service industries can be widely distributed across the continent. It will, at the same time, enable monetary operations to move seamlessly across the Union and help service companies to expand their activities to all corners of Europe, secure in the knowledge that they work within standardized rules. And not least it will protect individual citizens of the Union, no matter where they live and with which trans-national company they enter into any agreement.'

What I feel Lydia and her friends, who are so inclined to resort to regulations, fail to understand is that money has always had a magical, almost spiritual fluidity. It runs to the point where it can be used and finds a route past every obstacle. The history of modern Europe is the history of this strange commodity, which is always restless, always seeking, and always at large. It is the commodity that Europe created, the great gift of those Venetian, Genoan and Florentine pioneers who saw that you could cast this bread on the waters and that it would return after many days. International finance is not located, as construction work, agriculture or even scholarship are located. It takes place in the mysterious sphere where money resides – in figures and messages whose only permanent home is cyber-space, money flowing through institutions to where it can be most fruitfully used. What makes the City of London the financial *location* that it is, is not its geographical position but its place on the mental chessboard of competence and trust. Half of European financial transactions take place through London-based offices; and if those offices lose their competitive edge this critical source of wealth will leave Europe altogether. Forcing the City of London down regulatory channels that constrict its natural and self-regulating movements will benefit no-one in the EU. But it will give Wall Street and Zurich cause to rejoice. The integrationist approach to regulation threatens the very thing that made Europe into one of the world's financial centres.

The EU's inability to deal adequately with money matters is, of course, best exemplified by the administration of its revenue and expenditure. Its failure to produce competent accounts that could be passed by independent auditors is not in dispute. The greater part of the problem does not lie with the corruption within the works of the Commission itself, although that is bad enough. It is mainly due to the shambles in the accounting of funds dispensed by Brussels for various projects that are all administered through national governments. The sound financial management of their own non-profit making projects is difficult enough for these governments. It is doubly so when it is not their own money that is being spent but that of the Union. Acting as mere middlemen between the Commission and the various beneficiaries, national administrations are accountable to nobody; so it is hardly surprising that the accounts never add up. A naive Dutch bystander, unfamiliar with the convoluted intricacies of the EU budget, may well ask why money collected in the Netherlands should be re-routed via Brussels to fund works in a region of his own country. For it does not take an accountant to know that the more hands through which money travels the less of it remains.

The more fundamental question affects the entire structure of the built-in decision-making: the size of the EU budget, its objective and its use. The total monies available are determined by a meeting of representatives from 27 countries with the help of the Commission. Almost by definition, the Commission and the recipient countries must always want more money, whilst the donors prefer to spend their taxpayers' contributions on their own people. This conflict of interest is aggravated by the arcane method of calculating the proportional share of Member States' gains and losses. For good historical reasons, although the calculation is roughly based on respective GDPs, it is impossible to know the outcome and invariably subject to bitter disputes among Member States with conflicting national interests ahead of time. It produces wonderful anomalies like Luxemburg, the wealthiest nation *per capita*, being the greatest beneficiary. The objective of the budget has never been strategically defined. Support of rural life, regional regeneration, improvement of infrastructure, redistribution of wealth, research and development, overseas aid – these are all vying with each other for a share of the pot, without any comparative criteria as to the greatest common European good. Amidst all this uncertainty, the one constant factor is the continued accumulation of power and control in the centre.

Lydia knows these facts as well I do, but she pins her hopes on a reform of the system, the need of which, she says, is universally acknowledged and constantly discussed at each European summit. But a structure that originated with the purpose of subsidizing the French farmer, and has survived serious attempts at reform, requires radical surgery to make it fit for purpose. In my own view, if the single overriding objective is to transfer resources from the wealthier to the poorer Member States, the donor states should decide what they are prepared to contribute, and proportional amounts would be subject to a

statistical formula strictly based on relative GDPs. The best use
of such resources would be a matter for the recipient governments accountable only to their own electorate. Such a reform
would have the advantages of simplicity, transparency and palpable fairness, as well as actually reducing the Union's central
powers. I realize, however, that this is not what most of the
current European political leadership has in mind.

The matters that I have touched on in this letter are of special significance, since they illustrate the way in which Europe,
under the regime of central regulation imposed by the Commission, is being steadily decoupled from the global economy.
Whether we praise globalization as a liberating force, or condemn it as the death of small-scale dealings, globalization is a
fact. Transactions can now move around the world to the place
that best promotes them. And if that place is never Europe,
then Europe will enter a period of rapid and maybe terminal
decline. The EU institutions, born at a time when people could
seriously think that 'coal and steel' were the essential core of
economic life, belong to another world — one that has disap-
peared forever. My concern is that the European Union itself,
welded into that steel corset constructed over 50 years, should
not follow in its wake.

LETTER 5

Defending Society and Protecting the Individual

Lydia believes that the European idea of citizenship has a protective side. It takes seriously the view that every individual matters, and that it is a public duty, and therefore a duty of government, to ensure that all citizens are provided for. For Lydia, 'it is part of our European identity that we make the plight of the poor, the sick, the unemployed, the old and the homeless a matter of public concern. And what decent European would want to sacrifice that charitable inheritance for yet more wealth at the top of society, yet more economic growth, yet more consumption of wasteful and unnecessary commodities? Why not sacrifice a portion of economic growth for the far greater moral benefit of social protection? After all, a social model of European inspiration exists everywhere in Europe, even in countries following the Anglo-Saxon model of capitalism. It is one of the strengths of Europe in today's globalized world that it manages successfully to reconcile economic development with social progress and solidarity. Each country developed its own interpretation of the European social model over the course of its history. In some cases, this coincided with the development of the nation state itself. Indeed, the welfare state has been an important bond of loyalty between the citizen and the state. The resulting social systems, social bargaining structures and taxation schemes are highly centralized at national level. Today, they sometimes stand in the way of European integration and the implementation of the four freedoms of the internal market. How can we encourage the free movement of people to and from all European countries if labour law differs widely, if healthcare standards are uneven at best, if the portability of pensions is far from being realized? So, even though the European social model exists in every country, there is a need for agreeing on common standards and practices. Nation states have to relinquish some of their jealously guarded prerogatives in this domain for the ultimate benefit of all European citizens.'

As always Lydia has a point. And she is backed by the EC, which has been doing its best since the Presidency of Jacques Delors, a Socialist, to emphasize the 'European Social Model' as the defining achievement of the Union. However, in the future Europe that I envisage, in which sovereignty remains with the nation states, there will be no *European* social model. Different states will deal with health, unemployment, housing and pensions according to their own prescriptions. Long-standing deals between government and unions, expectations regarding benefits, retirement age and the provision of health services will vary from country to country, and each government will have to work out its own way of answering to the needs of its poorer citizens. And each social model will bring with it a cost in the form of taxation and public expenditure. Without dissenting from Lydia's view, that we Europeans regard the poor and the needy as our collective responsibility, I believe that we shall discover the way to fulfil our social responsibilities effectively only if we allow the kind of free competition between social models that the EU seems bent on eliminating.

I say this, not out of commitment to any particular social model, but because I fear for the future of Europe if the promises made to its people cannot be met. Only by free competition between rival social models will we discover how best to reconcile extensive welfare provisions with the economic growth needed to sustain them. The current tendency within the Union is to take the Scandinavian system as an ideal, then covertly try to impose a uniform, high-tax model across the Union, with tough regulations binding the hands of employers, and benefits to employees that radically reduce the incentive to work. It is neither appropriate, nor acceptable to countries with an altogether different economic ethos. In the view of many thinkers and political movements across Europe, such a policy threatens to undermine the workings of the market in an area where only the market can deliver the resources necessary to make any social policy work.

The controversy here goes deep, and is itself part of our European heritage. There are those for whom the goal of social policy is to advance the cause of equality – meaning material and social equality between the citizens, so that the gap between rich and poor, economically powerful and powerless, successes and failures, is narrowed as much as possible. While the evidence for the free economy that influenced so many of the EU's founding fathers is indisputable, in some quarters, residual hostility to capitalism, and a belief that resources in the hands of the State are more likely to be directed to the public good than resources in the hands of individual entrepreneurs, remain. Such was the view of Jacques Delors; it is one that is shared by social democrats in Germany, France and Spain, and by the vestigial communist and socialist parties across Europe.

For others, the purpose of social policy is not the achievement of equality (other than equality before moral and legal judgement), but the abolition of need. No matter that some are richer, more powerful, more successful than others, provided that their wealth can be used to raise their needy fellows from indigence, to provide them with the goods, the incentives and the opportunities to live fulfilled and satisfying lives. When Ludwig Erhard proposed the 'social market' as the model for Europe, he was clear that the first step towards helping the needy is to institute a free economy. In reply to a query he said 'when I talk of the social market economy, I mean that the market is social, not that it needs to be made social.' Only in this way, he argued, could we liberate our most important economic resources, which are human enterprise, human labour and human creativity.

The tension between those two approaches exists in every European society, and it would be foolish to take final and definitive sides. Nevertheless, some factual comparisons are relevant. Countries like France and Germany, which have followed the Scandinavian model, with extensive state provision of benefits and with employment laws strongly biased in favour of the employee, have a relatively poor unemployment record. The contrary is true of countries like Britain and Ireland, in which low taxation is combined with relative freedom of employers to hire and fire their workforce whilst employees are encouraged to supplement the state provision with private health insurance and private pension funds. In 2005, unemployment in the EU was lowest in Ireland and Britain at around 4%, highest in France and Germany at around 9%. Yet more significant is the 'unemployment trap' that ensues when high taxation combined with high unemployment benefits effectively destroy the incentive to work. In Sweden, someone going from unemployment to a job paying 1500 euro a month increases his income by only 5 euro a day – and that increase is usually absorbed by meal and travel costs. Not surprisingly, therefore, Sweden has a growing long-term unemployment problem. An innovative way to reconcile the two opposing approaches is the Danish model of

'Flexicurity', combining flexible labour law with benefits and energetic job placement.

The free market model followed by Britain and Ireland seems to perform better when it comes to lifting people out of poverty. Between 1995 and 2004, the real income of the poorest 10% grew 78.6% in Ireland, 59.2% in Britain, 19.2% in the rest of the EU, and just 9.7% in Sweden. Following a change in government, Swedish policies are in fact moving away from the 'Scandinavian model', a sign that comparative judgements are relevant and influential, and that the adoption by the EU of a single model for all Member States will impede the process of adjustment.

Of course, statistics must be taken in context, and many will argue that the enhanced sense of social equality engendered by the Scandinavian model is worth the fiscal cost of it. My argument does not depend upon endorsing either the egalitarian or the entrepreneurial conception of welfare. I wish merely to say that the only way forward in this delicate matter is through trial and error, and that trial and error means diversity. Let each Member State pursue its own social model, and reap the benefits and the costs of it. Let us only be aware that money in the hands of the State is not necessarily money devoted to the public good, that the more the State seeks to provide, the higher the taxes, and the higher the taxes the lower the incentive to earn. The interesting corollary to this – the old observation (most recently associated with Laffer) that, beyond a certain point, higher taxes means lower receipts – has now been confirmed in Germany and Sweden. And in the UK, in 2007, opinion polls showed 90% believed that the money which the state poured into public services in the previous decade had been wasted. The worst thing the EU could do, therefore, is to impose a regulatory regime that would prevent Germany, Sweden or Britain from changing course.

Lydia laughed, as, to my surprise, she agreed. 'It is ironic that the EU is simultaneously attacked for wanting to install a pan-European socialist regime *and* declaring all-out war on the provisions of the welfare state. Clearly, there has to be some misunderstanding here, as both goals are mutually exclusive!' She asserted her trust in competition, and in the strength of diversity. She admitted that our collective social systems are in need of overhaul, to live up to the expectations of European citizens. But, she maintained that, for this, we have to adopt best practices at European level: 'The European Commission is well placed to guide this process of learning from our peers. With a Union of 27 members, countries cannot reach the same level of wealth and re-distributive possibilities overnight. We have seen this with prior enlargements: Greece, Spain and Portugal took 20 to 30 years to catch up, and the Union helped financially to accelerate the process. So, a little patience is needed for full convergence of degrees of social protection to be realized.

People are fearful of the destruction of their welfare state and the abolition of cherished social provisions. The EU has to be sensitive to these anxieties. If inspected closely, there is indeed a certain imbalance inherent in the structure of the European Community with the Single Market at its core. While many economic matters are centralized at the European level, everything 'social' outwardly remains the domain of the nation state, but heavily influenced by the inherent dynamic of the common market. A balance needs to be struck between the principle of competition and the notion of protective measures to safeguard the cohesion of European societies. Are we going to increase growth by increasing inequality following the Anglo-Saxon model or should we find a different way taking greater account of the social factor in supporting a more limited growth? The priority of the Single Market has to be stable societies that are both safe and happy. The EU has a mandate to strive for social and territorial cohesion of Europe. This is what its citizens expect.

European integration creates facts on the ground forcing us both to react and to be pro-active. It really depends on how we see Europe evolve and what tasks it is expected to take on in the future. When asked, citizens express a strong wish for the EU to become more active in areas outside its current mandate – managing globalization; combating unemployment; reforming the welfare state, especially pension systems; caring for the elderly. Just an example: in the EU, 80 million people, or 30% of wage earners, are currently unqualified workers at risk of losing their jobs to low-skilled labour around the world. Add to this a fast ageing society and you have an immediate need for action. In order to keep EU production levels up, that population will have to be retrained. The underlying belief seems to be that nation states on their own can no longer cope, that Europe needs to shoulder more responsibility even going beyond setting common standards. So it is conceivable that one day European budgetary funds might be made available to cushion asymmetric shocks in parts of Europe to compensate for loss of employment and to encourage retraining. Who knows? Maybe one day, a European-wide system of pensions and health care will secure the well-being of all individuals anywhere on the continent.'

Lydia's vision is superficially attractive. In its abstract terms, few would object to any of it. And indeed it is not beyond the realm of possibility that one day her dream will become a reality. But the way the EU is going about it, forcing the pace of integration by generating a flow of standardized regulations, that day is not coming any nearer. However, the package of social, financial, educational and health provision is only one aspect of the protection offered to the citizen by the state. That is as far as economic protection can go.

Equally important is the protection of the individual under the law. Criminal law and criminal procedure differ across the continent, and, again, the differences matter very much to those affected by them. In English law (Common law), the medieval writ of *habeas corpus*, declared to be a fundamental right of the subject in the Bill of Rights of 1689, still dominates criminal procedure. It has been qualified by recent anti-terrorist measures, but its main provision remains, namely, that nobody can be held for more than a minimal period without charge, and that criminal investigations must precede detention, and not begin with it. The medieval institution of trial by jury also survives in Britain, and is often held forth, along with *habeas corpus*, as a guarantee that the law belongs to the citizen, and not to the state. Defenders of the *Code Napoléon* react by pointing to the difficulty in securing convictions under English law, and the near impossibility of extraditing terrorists, some of whom are wanted in France for multiple murders. Freedoms enjoyed by criminals, they may argue, are freedoms stolen from the citizen, and the real test of a criminal system is not to be measured by the freedom of those who might be prosecuted, but by the security of the law-abiding majority whose peace they disturb. Many continental legal systems, rooted in Roman law, have built-in provisions for the protection of the individual *vis-à-vis* the state. These not only differ from those furnished by Common law, they also differ significantly from each other. These differences are deeply embedded and, I believe, it is perilous to try to override them.

Lydia has another perspective: 'It is true that the European Union is becoming more active in areas such as justice and home affairs that were once the sole prerogative of the nation state. This is merely a natural consequence of the dynamics of the internal market and its four freedoms. The EU is forced to react to protect the European citizen from potential nega-

tive fall-outs. We need no reminder of growing cross-border crime and the acute danger of terrorism. This is why the
Charter of Fundamental Rights, signed by all Member States
at the European Council meeting in Nice in 2000, is so vital.
Let me simply quote from its Preamble: "Conscious of its spiritual and moral heritage, the Union is founded on the indivis-
ible, universal values of human dignity, freedom, equality and
solidarity; it is based on the principles of democracy and the
rule of law. It places the individual at the heart of its activities,
by establishing the citizenship of the Union and by creating an
area of freedom, security and justice." To bind the authorities
of the Member States and of the Community, organs, rights and
freedoms of the individual are thus enshrined and protected.
These standards are minimum standards and should be binding
for all present and future Member States. They tell us and others what we stand for.'

The principles to which Lydia is attached are formulated
with eloquence in the preambles to many of the Union's treaties. They are, however, so general that no one can take issue
with them. In practice, in the detail of the real world, criminal
procedure and policing are experienced by the ordinary citizen
as an intimate part of the deal that binds him to the state; to
alter them is to meddle with deep-seated feelings of legitimacy.
Even if we believe that the fight against terrorism and organized
crime requires extensive cooperation across national frontiers,
we must respect the diverse frameworks of criminal justice
established in the Member States. Like the diverse frameworks
of social security, they touch on the felt reality of citizenship,
and to meddle with them is to jeopardize the sentiments on
which all political order depends.

Such is not the attitude taken by the EU, whose *Corpus Juris*
proposals are now likely to be introduced under Section 280 of
the Treaty of Amsterdam. These proposals involve establishing

a European Public Prosecutor Service (EPP), with powers to request that someone be remanded in custody for up to six months, renewable for a further three months, where there are reasonable grounds to suspect that he has committed an offence or even 'good reasons to believe it necessary to stop him committing such an offence'. Article 26(1) says that courts must consist of professional judges, and not simply jurors or lay magistrates, while 'in the case of partial or total acquittal appeal is also open to the EPP as a prosecuting party'. In other words, suspects can be tried twice for the same offence. In short, the proposals amount to the partial abolition of the protections offered to the accused under the English criminal law system, and the undoing of many centuries of English jurisprudence. If the proposals are introduced they will lead to an unstoppable surge of hostility towards the EU not only in Britain, but also in other countries that rightly feel the EU to be trampling on national legal safeguards put in place to protect the individual.

Although Lydia may disagree, I am convinced that the diversity of legal cultures on the continent offers far greater protection to the individual within a national framework than within a newly created, standardized, untried, pan-European system. This does not mean that some countries which share a similar legal tradition should be discouraged from harmonizing their laws. But such integration should not be based on uneasy compromises and certainly never binding on all Member States.

Law

For Lydia, harmonization of the economic and social model necessarily engages harmonization of legal practice. Since law is the way in which a society speaks to itself about its identity, this issue of European law is not merely one of technical convenience. It is fundamental; the leading means to abolish the old violence of international dispute resolution. So the EU is attempting to form a genuinely supranational jurisdiction, a system of law that can operate impartially across frontiers, defining rights and duties that are as recognizable in Spain as they are in Sweden. If successful, this would enable people to settle their conflicts by the only way that has a real track-record of settling conflicts peacefully, namely through a court of law. Lydia admits that European law at first glance indeed looks like a strange creature – a new form of international law. 'But its unique supranational character allows it to operate harmoniously alongside the laws of European Member States. EU law is quite fitting for the hermaphrodite that is the European Union – neither a federal state nor an intergovernmental organization. This permanent compromise is mirrored in the European

legal order providing both the necessary structure and indispensable flexibility.'

Moreover, according to Lydia, European law acquired a natural supremacy over national laws because it is an expression
of the common will of the nations of Europe who signed the
treaties founding the European Communities and the European
Union. Creating unity and consistency throughout a big geographical and thematic expanse had to result in the loss of some
state prerogatives and rights. 'The concept of primacy is nothing
intellectually new if you come from a country with a federal
tradition. But European law shapes not only form and content
of the internal market, of the "Common Foreign and Security
Policy" and of "Police and Judicial Co-operation", respectively
the three pillars of the European Union. It makes us who we are,
a community of shared values. Law is how we articulate that.'

Lydia rather dislikes the emphasis on economics, not only
because it risks distorting the real message of the Union, but
also because it tends to skew the political process, tying the
European project to the consumerist attitudes that it ought
to be transcending. But she accepted, as a necessary evil, Jean
Monnet's stratagem of beginning the road to integration with
the least overtly political areas, pre-eminently economics, the
ends justifying the means. But her unvarnished view is that the
European project works, she says, only if it is attached to genuine ideals. To justify it in purely materialist terms is not to
justify it, but to condemn it. Europe, in her eyes, is first and
foremost an object of belief not of appetite. And if you cannot
believe in it, then it is best to forget it.

I agree with Lydia. But I cannot help thinking that her
emphasis on law identifies a weakness, and not a strength in the
existing project. It is perhaps more obviously true of law than
it is of any other human institution, that it must be informed by
an ethos of accountability. Judges must be accountable for their

judgments and legislators for their laws. And if the people have no say in how those laws are made or how they should be limited, then the legitimacy of the law is put in question. Without venturing too far into political theory, it is safe to assert that, if there is a reason above all others to praise the civilization of Europe, it lies in the emergence on this continent of a rule of law, in which law stands higher than those who make it and holds them to account. The 'empire of laws, not of men' was no innovation of John Adams, but an ideal already defended in the *Politics* of Aristotle, an ideal implicit in the Institutes and Digest of Justinian, and one to which the thinkers of the Middle Ages and the Renaissance returned again and again.

It is precisely for this reason that law, in Europe, has been connected with national sovereignty. Law, for us, is the law of the land. And although many of our legal systems derive in large measure from what was, originally, the universal jurisprudence of Roman law, they have evolved in different ways in different places, and incorporated into themselves the legacy of national history. It should be remembered that the laws which survive in any state are not those made in times of war or other emergency, but those made in times of peace. The legal systems of Europe contain within themselves – and especially in what pertains to civil association – the legacy of peace, and the formula for re-establishing peace after any conflict. To interfere with their operation, or to over-ride their provisions with edicts that are not responsive to the deep sediments of argumentation that they contain, is to put at risk the most important source of stability in the European communities. Lydia is right to see our legal inheritance as one of the proudest of European achievements; but for that very reason she ought to be wary of the EU's attempt to smother that inheritance under a mass of decrees that pay no respect to the many ways in which European laws have hitherto been made.

The European nation states have been governed throughout their existence by territorial rules of law and it is this attachment of law to territory, rather than religion, that is the ultimate source of European liberties. The legal systems of the European nation states are, therefore, proof of the underlying unity of Europe. But they are also proof of its diversity. Even among those states which adopted, whether willingly or by force, the *Code Napoléon*, subsequent evolution, through case law and statute, has caused their legal systems to grow apart, so that each is indelibly marked by the national character and national history that it has been designed to serve. Compare the law of Italy as it is today with that of France, and both with their shared Napoleonic ancestor, and you will see how a living legal tradition enshrines deep-rooted ways of doing things, enduring attitudes to social conflict and its resolution, and the evolving requirements of institutions rooted in the soil of the country.

Yet more striking, of course, is the contrast between the Common law of England and the codified laws of most continental countries. The law of England has evolved over the past millennium or more from the interaction between local custom – ultimately the Common law – and the common interest embodied in Statute law. Judges have held the balance of interpretation throughout the latter and more peaceable parts of this period; and settled law now resides in the unappealed judgments of the highest adjudicating Court. Common law incorporates a principle of finality, that matters can become *res judicata* – settled matters – which rests on the doctrine of *stare decisis* – that particular decisions should stand unaltered. Such decisions have the status of 'precedents', which must be followed wherever they apply. They can be overruled by a higher court or by a statute. But those higher sources must be read as contributions to an organic system of law, each part of which is dependent on every other. To discover the law, therefore, the judge will have to delve into the concrete details of former cases, animated always by the belief that there *is* a law that settles them, but often not knowing in advance what it is. There is a constant and creative tension between case law and statute.

Those brought up on Roman law or the *Code Napoléon* find this astonishing, since they see law as a deductive system, beginning from first principles, and working downwards to the particular case from a legislated text, formed and given to the citizen by the state. But my English friends assure me that Common law can be explained easily enough, once you see that it expresses a characteristically English attitude to social order. Common law arose not from edicts of the sovereign, dictating rules to his subjects, but from the subjects' search for *remedies*. A person who has suffered a wrong, whether from a private individual or from the sovereign himself, would petition the sovereign's justices for a remedy. When the medieval courts were unable to provide a remedy from their store of precedents and procedures, subjects would petition the sovereign directly, through the court of Chancery. And thus arose the auxiliary system of 'equity', from which in turn arose that peculiar invention, the 'trust'.

From my Scottish merchant father, I have learned enough of the Common law to make it obvious that such a system is radically different from, and incommensurate with, the deductive system administered by the French *Cour de cassation* or the mountainous book of rulings administered by the European Court of Justice (ECJ). Common law is constructed from the bottom up. It is binding on the sovereign, since it consists in the remedies that the courts have offered in his name; and it can avoid unjust edicts through the 'doctrines of equity', which produce those marvellous intellectual constructs such as trust, beneficial ownership and injunction (which, by the way, are partly responsible for the pre-eminence of England in the world of finance). In all kinds of ways, Common law resists dictatorship, and even if it is also a rule of Common law that the courts apply all statutes according to 'the will of Parliament', it is for the courts, not Parliament, to discern what that will might be. Since judiciary procedure rooted in Common law responds immediately to grievances, it has made the top-down regulation of commerce largely unnecessary. Product liability, for example, governed in continental systems by massive regulation, was, until entry into the European Union, largely governed in English law by the leading case of *Donoghue v. Stevenson* of 1932, in which someone made ill by a decomposed snail which had found its way into a ginger-beer bottle successfully sued the manufacturer. The case made it clear that the rule of Common law is not, as in Roman law, *caveat emptor,* but rather *caveat vendor* – let the vendor take note of his duty of care towards all those who can reasonably be expected to encounter his product.

Not surprisingly, therefore, national law, be it Common or continental, sits uneasily with the law of the EU. It goes entirely against the grain of national jurisprudence to believe that a regulation issued from Brussels is *already* part of the law of the land. The legislative powers conferred on the Council of Ministers by the Treaty of Rome were perhaps not intended, at the time, to issue in such a flood of edicts as to become responsible for most of the legislation adopted by the assemblies and parliaments of the Member States. So it is not only the Common law of England that bridles against this top-down approach to legislation. The laws of the European states are either discovered, like Common law, in the intricacies of social conflict, or adopted by elected assemblies after open discussion and the published deliberations of committees. In all the national systems of law, the attempt has been made to fit law to the perceived social needs of the nation, and to solicit the consent of the people not merely law by law but case by case, through the workings of the courts.

In contrast, the edicts of the Council of Ministers are issued after unminuted discussions held in secret, on the basis of proposals made by the bureaucrats of the Commission, guided by principles in which the limits to legislation are not clearly stated or publicly rehearsed. Yet, under the doctrine of 'shared competence', it is held that where the EU and a Member State both have the right to legislate in a certain area, the Member State's right ceases just as soon as the EU decides to exercise its competence. In such a case, the Commission's edicts override all countervailing laws of the Member States, whatever the opposing strength of jurisprudential opinion. So it has been held in the landmark case of *Factortame v The United Kingdom*, in which the ECJ effectively overruled the House of Lords, and struck down an important act of the UK Parliament (the Merchant Shipping Act 1988). And so it was assumed in the Vaxholm case, which pitted European free-movement legislation against some of the most fundamental of Swedish employment laws, the very laws which established a regime of collective bargaining that Europe considers part of its 'social model'. On 18 December 2007, the ECJ upheld European legislation, *de facto* wiping out a legal inheritance which represents decades of compromise and bargaining, and which is fundamental to the character of post-war Swedish society. Nor is a Member State protected from this legal predation by its Constitution. In 2005, the German Constitutional Court ruled the EU Arrest Warrant unconstitutional.* Instead of bowing to the Court, the politicians who had signed up to this particularly objectionable provision passed a new law in 2006 taking into account elements admonished by the Constitutional Court.

---

* In its 1993 Maastricht Decision, the German Federal Constitutional Court enshrines its final say over European law and a national obligation to disobedience if EU law is in violation of the German Constitution.

The problem here lies deep within the structure of the European Union. Laws passed as a result of EU regulations and Directives are not merely adopted by the legislatures of the Member States. They are effectively subsumed under the Treaties, and therefore made irreversible. The most basic rule of law-making – that mistakes can be unmade – is absent from the European legal process. At the same time, the ECJ, which is supposed to rule on all conflicts created by the European legislation, is expressly called upon to advance the project of 'ever closer union', and will, therefore, in any case where judicial discretion or innovation is needed, look to that project for its guiding principle. This is, indeed, required of it, by the EU's doctrine demanding the 'sincere mutual cooperation' of institutions within the Union. The point has been made many times by Professor Ronald Vaubel of the University of Mannheim, a member of the Academic Advisory Council to the German Federal Ministry of Economics. As he puts it, 'the parliaments may try to defend their competencies at the European Court of Justice, but the Court shares the vested interest of the other European institutions in centralizing power at the Union level'. Furthermore, the very process that ties European law to the Treaties also deprives the Court of penalties. Fines are offset by the financial gain from disobedience and the only sanction with a genuinely deterrent effect – expulsion from the Union – is one that cannot be contemplated, given that non-complying Member States will simply act as though the threat could never be carried out.

Not only does the regime of European legislation fit uneasily with the sovereign claims of national parliaments, and with the authority of the courts of law. The EU institutions have now begun to assume the right to harmonize criminal law and legal procedure across the continent. This, it seems to me, is the most dangerous initiative of all, and one that will throw the unpopularity of the European institutions into the sharpest relief. Vaguely defined criminal offences (racism and xenophobia, for instance), backed up by continent-wide powers of extradition, and procedures based on the system that prevails in Italy, Spain and France, will inevitably alienate the British and Scandinavian peoples, whose native laws do not recognize the relevant offences, and who have an understandable objection to being extradited to places where you can be held without trial at the *juge d'instruction*'s pleasure.

The ECJ has in fact already ruled (Case C-176/03, September 2005, Protection of the Environment through Criminal Law) that the EU is able to propose criminal sanctions in all areas of 'Community competence'. And the Commission has proposed that the Member States should use the so-called *passerelle*, or 'footbridge', clause of the Maastricht Treaty in order to bring criminal justice and policing into the sphere of 'Community competence'. The Commission wants to unify criminal procedure across the continent. The effect of this would be to transfer final judgment in some criminal trials to the ECJ, which takes up to two years to rule on a case. This could force national governments to hold suspects in custody for two years pending judgment, something inconceivable in the Northern Member States.

I spoke at length and Lydia, to her credit, listened patiently while I got deeply felt things off my chest. Then she set about trying to calm my agitated thoughts. In essence, this is what she said: 'Your love for your father's legal tradition does you great credit. Let me nevertheless point out a few misconceptions clouding your judgement. You mentioned the Common law principle of *stare decisis*. It is true that in continental law, court judgments are taken into account only *inter pares*. Nevertheless, the continental system also uses case law (writs of higher courts) to interpret and qualify laws voted by parliament. These decisions form part of the body of the law, are binding and have to be taken into account every time a judicial decision is made from then on. Laws, once adopted, can be interpreted following different methodologies – grammatical, historical and teleological. Usually, in the "old" EU countries, teleological interpretation is preferred, following the will of the legislator and, as a second benchmark, the constitution. Courts can disregard laws if they find them to be in violation of important principles of the respective legal order. From a continental perspective, it is laws – transparent and applicable for everyone – which act as reliable guarantors of equal treatment, proportionality and equity, not reliance on cases. But you overplay the differences, Publia. For example, in contractual relations, the Roman law principle of *caveat emptor* has long been superseded by the principle of *bona fides*, "good faith", protecting the buyer even in the negotiation phase of a contract. It is interesting to note that this key principle of the Roman *lex mercatoria* has greatly influenced the English commercial contract tradition. I think that, in essence, continental law is based on the same principles of trust, beneficial ownership and equity as Common law. We are actually much closer than you would like to have it.

What we see in Europe today is a sort of osmosis of different legal traditions both of the Common law-inspired and the so-called "continental" legal systems that make up the EU. The ECJ itself has enshrined the importance of case law, which should make Common law countries rejoice. In many legal fields, be it administrative (public) law, or business (private) law, we see a movement of European convergence, through comparative law, exchange of opinion among jurists and national jurisdiction looking abroad and to the ECJ for guidance.

European law, also referred to as the Community *acquis*, is complex. It comprises founding treaties and legislative acts derived from them (including framework decisions of the

Council), as well as general principles of law, the case law of the Court of Justice, international agreements signed by the Community and supplementary law contained in conventions and agreements between Member States. Interpretation of this body of European law by the ECJ is seen by some as promoting the smooth functioning of the EU, by others as interfering with national sovereignty. Rudolf von Jhering, a distinguished German 19th-century jurist, first articulated the concept of jurisprudence based on teleological principles. What purpose does law serve? I am of the opinion that the ECJ, over the course of its brief history, has faithfully interpreted the constituent treaties, as well as the rest of the *acquis*. Yes, it has chosen a teleological approach as outlined in the preamble of the Treaty of Rome. Yes, in years of stagnation, it has been a motor of integration, and we all should be thankful for that. If not for the Court, who would have fought for the rights of European citizens, who would have put in place the building blocks of the common market, who would have kept the European spirit alive? Without it, those would have been lost years.

Building an internal market mirroring the complexities of modern economic life must have repercussions in the field of "Justice and Home Affairs", yes, even in criminal law. Eurojust, composed of prosecutors, magistrates and senior police officers, was set up five years ago on demand of the Member States in order to coordinate the fight against cross-border crime throughout Europe. To fulfil its mandate, it has to be given powers to issue arrest warrants, seize goods and order prosecutions. A European public prosecutor is essential for directing national police forces when dealing with cross-border crimes, counter-terrorism and fraud.

A word on subsidiarity, cornerstone to a harmonious construction of Europe, as we both agree. Have you noticed that our politicians like to sing two different tunes on the subject?

On Sundays, they praise the sovereignty of the nation state deploring EU interventionism, and on Mondays, they turn to the European Commission demanding immediate action in fields as varied as football hooliganism and energy policy. You cannot have it both ways. It is time to admit that the EU, and consequently European law, exist because nation states cannot solve problems on their own anymore. What is law but "coagulated politics"? If politicians do not provide guidance for the direction of the EU, it is not surprising that judges could be tempted to jump into the fray. It is up to decision-makers to put their house in order, rather than conveniently blaming European institutions. However, I believe a certain tacit "balance of terror" already exists between the European institutions, especially the ECJ and the Member States, not to advance into territory deemed "culturally" sensitive at national level.'

In her book on the federal idea (one of the foundation textbooks at the College of Europe in Bruges), Lydia lays great emphasis on the doctrine of human rights, which she holds to be the only lasting foundation of peace in the modern world. She also argues that the European institutions are bound by the European Convention on Human Rights, and will therefore always offer whatever safeguards are necessary to ensure the freedom and rights of the individual. She drew my attention to the argument which I read with interest, but also with a measure of scepticism. It has been apparent at least since the French Revolution that rights are not always protected by the institutions that declare them, and that, in any case, the habit of declaring rights is as likely to create conflicts as to resolve them. A conflict in the courts is a zero-sum game, with a winner and a loser. The rights thereby conferred cannot be diminished, brokered or qualified in the interests of the losing party. By contrast, a conflict put before a legislative assembly is one with a compromise solution.

Of course, Lydia is fully aware that, in implementing regulations and Directives, the European landscape is most uneven. Where we differ is what that holds for the future. She believes that there have been huge improvements in recent years and, even if norms are not transposed into national law immediately, principles have a tendency to develop normative vigour and efficacy over time; whereas I am convinced of the opposite. Left to take its present course, European jurisdiction will fragment on its own, leading to a disorderly and uncontrolled disintegration of the political continent. So, in my view, the principal law-making functions, those to do with criminal law, civil conflicts, the ownership of land and property, planning and local administration, must be retained by national parliaments and national courts. The powers allotted to European institutions have to be transferred under a process that is entirely transparent to the people affected. As for the ECJ, its role and scope must be strictly limited to disputes arising under the Treaties as approved at any given time. To allow it to improvise, guided only by a project – 'ever closer union' – which is neither legally defined nor practically obtainable, is to jeopardize all the legislative traditions of our continent.

Reflecting on our exchange, I concluded that, whereas we find agreement or compromise in other matters, in this area, Lydia and I cannot resolve such a fundamental divergence of beliefs, despite Lydia's kind attempts to minimize our differences. Perhaps they reflect an underlying fault line across the continent. Perhaps one single rigid framework cannot accommodate the political aspirations of all the European nations. If we are to preserve those areas where action at the European level is desirable, we need to find a more accommodating framework. Some countries will adopt common standards without forcing the whole Union to go along.

LETTER 7

Constitution

When Publius set out to persuade the citizens of New York to endorse the federal constitution of the United States, he affirmed from the start that their consent was the *sine qua non* of the document's validity. His tone was lofty and dignified. His concerns were the safety and freedom of the people. His intention was to show that the Constitution embodied the highest aspirations of those who had fought for their independence against the British crown. He argued that the document preserved the pre-existing liberties of the citizen, while balancing the powers of government so effectively against each other as to ensure that political decisions would represent no faction within the commonwealth, but rather the will of the people as a whole. Of course, it is one of the intricate questions of political philosophy whether a constitution could ever be devised that would have such a result – the result of creating genuine sovereignty, which is also a sovereignty of the people. But there is no doubt that Publius, whose education in these matters was a notch or two above the education of our current political class, had absorbed the arguments of Aristotle, Locke and Montesquieu, and recognized that a constitution exists not merely to create powers but also to limit them.

We have before us a signed 'Treaty of Lisbon – Amending the Treaty on European Union and the Treaty establishing the European Community' (*Official Journal of the European Union*, 2007/C 306/01). The reason for adopting such an unwieldy title is because the 'Treaty establishing a Constitution for Europe' (*Official Journal of the European Union*, 2004/C 310/01) has become discredited after rejection by the French and Dutch referenda in 2005. Notwithstanding, the creator of the Constitution, President Giscard d'Estaing, former President of France and a well-known advocate of European integration, has reassured the public that all essential features of his masterpiece have been preserved in the current text. He has also observed that, as a matter of fact, these features have been deliberately couched in unintelligible terms. He explained that the purpose (of which he said that he personally disapproved) was to obscure what has previously been more explicit.

The Lisbon Treaty is a remarkable document. It is the work not of political philosophers but of politicians and their co-opted civil servants – or maybe of civil servants and their co-opted politicians. The Convention that produced its predecessor document was set up in response to the 'Laeken Declaration' of 2001 by the heads of government of all the Member States. Its objective was to establish a more democratic, a more transparent process in Europe, purportedly setting unambiguous borderlines between the powers of the Member States and those of the Union. It is ten times the length of the American Constitution, and written in a language that is simultaneously ambiguous and imperative. There are many disagreements as to what this Constitution means and what it does, but there is no doubt that it fails in its primary objective. The dividing lines between the two sets of powers are left more opaque than

they are now. Instead of the crisp legal provisions of its American forerunner, in which rights, duties, procedures and powers
are clearly laid down and precisely limited, the Constitution
lights upon all the areas in which the European institutions
have acquired an interest, and prepares the way, through vague
language and barely judiciable procedures, for the indefinite
expansion of their powers.

In addressing the principle of subsidiarity, which is the guar-
antor of national sovereignty in European matters, the language
of the Treaty of Lisbon clearly implies that it is for the *Union*
to declare whether some matter can be sufficiently resolved
by the Member States: 'The Member States shall exercise their
competence to the extent that the Union has not exercised
its competence. The Member States shall again exercise their
competence to the extent that the Union has decided to cease
exercising its competence.'* True, the Lisbon Treaty, as well as
the Constitution, incorporates a protocol requiring EU institutions to show evidence, before taking charge of some matter,
that it cannot be dealt with adequately at the national level.
But the standard of proof is vague, and the arbiter appointed is
the ECJ, an institution committed to the project of 'ever closer
union'. Hence, the protocol merely removes the guarantees
that it purports to grant.

As in generality, so in specifics. Under 'Title I Categories
and Areas of Union Competence', Article 2 D-2, the Lisbon
Treaty tells us that 'the Union shall take measures to ensure
coordination of the employment policies of the Member States,
in particular by defining guidelines for these policies'.** This

---

* Title I 'Categories and Areas of Union Competence', Article 2 A-2
Lisbon Treaty, expressing the same idea as Part I, Title III 'Union Competences', Article I-11 Fundamental principles, Constitutional Treaty
** Formerly Part I, Title III 'Union Competences', Article I-15 The coordination of economic and employment policies, Constitutional Treaty

clause is sufficiently vague that it could be used, and certainly will be used, to authorize central control over every matter to do with employment: the hours of work, the age of retirement, the provision of pensions and the regulation of the workplace throughout the Union. Concealed within an ambiguous sentence, therefore, is a result which has been opposed for years at the inter-governmental level.

It is not my intention in this letter to examine all the ways in which the proposed Constitution and now Lisbon Treaty expropriates the powers of the Member States and concentrates them in the hands of the Commission. The point has been sufficiently argued by others. In what concerns the powers of the Union, the current document limits nothing and permits everything. In the crucial matters that touch on the residual rights of the Member States, it still makes only the vaguest attempt to meet the minimum requirements of those not committed to unbridled integration irrespective of consequence. The fact that the text envisages an enhanced role for the European Parliament still leaves the *acquis communautaire* intact. And it is precisely the *acquis* that wars against national autonomy, as it reveals in its very name: it is an irreversible process. It is a mechanism for removing powers from the Member States without the means of ever returning them.

It is at this point that we need to understand the word 'federal'. For Publius, a federal constitution describes the powers that are surrendered to the union by the states that compose it. Accordingly, all that is not explicitly surrendered by the Member States is retained by them. The extent of the surrender in the USA became a matter of dispute, leading to civil war. Its lesson has yet to be learned by the architects of a European project that ignores most diverse national interests. Nevertheless, the intention was clear: to delimit the powers and the procedures surrendered, and to withhold the remainder. With the European Constitution the intention is the opposite. The powers retained by the Member States are surrendered to *them*, on sufferance, by the central institutions. Everything belongs to the centre, except those 'subsidiary' powers allocated by a court that is itself a creature of the central power. It is a quite crucial – a defining – difference.

The integrationist conception of federalism echoes the *étatisme* of the French, who have never lost the vision of central government bequeathed to them by Louis XIV, and retained through the Revolutionary and Napoleonic periods, to form the backbone of the modern republic. And it is certainly true that the French conception of the state is very different from that of the German or the British. More than half of French GDP passes through the hands of the state, and more than half of all employees are on its payroll. France's entrenched bureaucracy enjoys aristocratic privileges and powers that are the envy of their counterparts among their European neighbours. Its ability to take executive action, without the consent of the elected politicians, the judiciary or the local mayors, far exceeds the democratic norm.

The post-war German Constitution, framed under strong American influence, was conceived on the model assumed by Publius, with the *Länder* retaining all powers that were not explicitly surrendered to the *Bundesrepublik*. And the British have got along with an unwritten constitution in which power is hidden within the workings of so many institutions that it is almost impossible to identify, at any moment, the entity that is entitled to exercise it. Some have even drawn the conclusion that, while the British and German constitutions are the means to generate consent, that of France is a means to impose the will of the state. And to a considerable extent history confirms this view of things. How otherwise do we explain the periodic revolutions, not to speak of seventeen successive constitutions and five

Republics, during the last two centuries of French history?

Nevertheless, we should recognize that it was the French people who were the first to reject the European Constitution when it was presented for their approval. They are no more content than the rest of Europe to see the steady expropriation of their decision-making powers by bureaucrats in another country with an agenda of their own. Look at the public pronouncements of the European Commission and try to find evidence of contrition, and you will look in vain. Following the 'No' votes of the French and the Dutch regarding the Constitutional Treaty, the EU and the government of France launched websites designed to prove that the people have always been consulted. But the websites are one continuous stream of propaganda, conveyed in the kind of Eurospeak that, like Orwell's Newspeak, makes heretical thoughts inexpressible. Furthermore, look at the treaties and their accompanying propaganda, and you will find only imperatives, timetables, declarations of what *must* be achieved by *when*, rather than appeals for popular consideration and open debate. Politicians sometimes speak of a 'fast track' and a 'slow track' into the European future: to a sceptical observer, however, the European process resembles a runaway train.

Lydia thought I was much too hard on the French and, since the entire European construction was initially built on the French model, by implication unfair to the now signed Constitution under the name of Lisbon Treaty. This is how she replied to my passionate plea: 'You are overreacting! Calm down, my friend. Apart from the eccentric English who have an allergy to written constitutions, the other European nations have always created substantive documents to enshrine the rights of the citizen and the state in relation to each other. These constitutions were held in high esteem because they provided the only protection for the individual as countries moved from arbitrary

feudal rule to democratic government. Some nations, especially France, might have become addicted to the constitution
business and created too many too frequently, but it is surely
better to have had too many than none at all?

Some people think that the step of preparing a constitution
for Europe might have been premature and they may well have
a point. Certainly, to give it such a grandiose treatment and
bestow on it such a monumental title was a grave tactical error.
After all, calling it a Constitutional Treaty has been a contradiction in terms. You are either dealing with a constitution or with
a treaty. A constitution is an ambitious document, aiming to
shape society through a long-term vision, something that was
not achieved with the document negotiated under the aegis of
Giscard d'Estaing, despite some flags and hymns. It might have
been better simply to amend the existing EU treaties in stages,
as we have done from summit to summit from the very beginning. We would have spared ourselves the vociferous and exaggerated reaction from forces bitterly opposed to any further
integration. On top of that, the pain of referenda, undoubtedly,
was an unnecessary diversion. Having learned our lesson, the
long-awaited Reform Treaty, negotiated in July and signed in
December 2007 as the Treaty of Lisbon, will simply confirm
and consolidate some elements already existing or underway.
Publia, you make great play of the close congruence between
the now buried constitution and the Lisbon Treaty. This entirely
misses the point – or maybe seeks to obscure it. As some MEP
said, the Lisbon Treaty might be 90-95% the same as the Constitutional Treaty, but biologically, we are 95% the same as
mice, and ultimately quite different.

The decision of the French and Dutch peoples, as we all
well know, had not much to do with the Constitution itself.
Nobody, not even the vast majority of parliamentarians, had
read the full text, never mind understood the crucial changes

needed to take the European project forward. Referenda, in any case, are highly questionable instruments of democracy. Reducing complex matters, such as the convoluted provisions of the EU, to a simple Yes/No question does not do justice to any meaningful consultation process between government and people. If you ask the man in the street across the continent how he would like to participate in the democratic process, he will tell you that such an activity is best left to politicians who are elected precisely to do this job. And, in my view, the man in the street is right: parliament is the best democratic instrument invented so far.

At last we are over the distracting debate about a constitution. The freshly signed Treaty of Lisbon will benefit future generations and, once the dust is settled, no-one will bother to ask how exactly it came about. The significant modifications of the Treaty of Maastricht and the substantial extensions of EU powers are simply the logical consequences of enlargement. Within the old rules, a Union of 27 countries and likely more in the future, decision-making becomes impossible, leading to paralysis. However, if we are serious about uniting Europe, it is a natural step in moving to something like a federal state in the future with a just and proper constitution.

But the point is that a constitution can create nothing new; it can only summarize our expectations. The American Constitution is not contained in the piece of paper that Publius defended. It is contained in the genius of the American people, in their customs, expectations and legal inheritance, to which Publius was appealing in his letters, and which he believed would prompt their consent to what was, in fact, no more than a written summary of their existing practices.'

I reflected on Lydia's riposte. There is something persuasive in the idea that the American Constitution began life as a summary of existing practices. But those practices were only

part of what made the Constitution possible. There was also
the shared way of life, shared language, shared legal system,
shared Anglo-Protestant culture, shared loyalty to the emerging nation; which between them caused that document to
command the understanding and sympathy of every educated
American. Alexis de Toqueville saw all this with astonishing
insight when he asked what made democracy in America possible in the 1840s. In sharp contrast, the European Constitution does not reflect any emerging loyalty to Europe, nor can
it rely on any embedded cultural, linguistic, legal or national
unity of the kind that made the United States of America possible. Lydia is surely right that a Constitution is or ought to be
rooted in existing expectations. And it must express the kind
of deep commitment that would persuade ordinary people to
be guided by it and to risk their lives on its behalf. Judged by
those exacting standards, the initially proposed Constitutional
Treaty and its confusing overcoat, the Reform Treaty or Lisbon Treaty, is a dismal failure. It bears no relation to the actual
behaviour of the people and the nations of Europe. It does not
summarize existing customs or expectations but is conceived
purely as a milestone towards a united future. It promises to
establish exact boundaries between areas of national and areas
of Union competence, but fails entirely to deliver on the promise. It claims to have the unanimous endorsement of the nations
and the people of Europe, but has no grounds whatsoever for
making the claim.

   Nor, it seems to me, are those defects merely faults of the
existing constitutional document. They belong to the very enterprise of the so-called Constitutional Treaty, which, as Lydia has
alluded to, is either a constitution or a treaty but which *cannot
be both*. A constitution means one sovereignty; a treaty means
several. A constitution appropriates powers; a treaty withholds
them. Given the historical, cultural and political diversity of

the European nations, there is no way in which a European Constitution could summarize and give legal protection to a common allegiance and a shared way of life. The best that we can hope for is a set of treaties that respect the sovereignty of the nation states, and enable their citizens to experience to the full those aspects of national loyalty, which resonate with the idea of Europe.

Here, as in the related and underlying matter of harmonization of legal traditions, the gulf between us, Lydia and I, was just too great to bridge. So we agreed to disagree. But as a practical measure, to cope with the current crisis, we both thought that those countries desiring to harmonize further their economic and political futures should not be hindered from doing so by those not wishing to travel that road.

LETTER 8

Regulation

In no matter has the European project had greater impact on the lives of ordinary Europeans than that of regulation. Most of the day-to-day grumbles against Brussels concern some or other new regulation judged to be insensitive, oppressive or unnecessary. The cost of European regulation to the economies of the Member States is now so great that even the European Commission believes that something must be done to reduce it. According to the EU Commission Vice-President responsible for Enterprise and Industry, the cost of EU regulations to the economies of Europe amounts to the combined GNP of Austria and the Netherlands. A recent study by Open Europe concludes that 77% of the cost of regulation on business in the UK since 1998 has been driven by EU legislation. Moreover, the British Federation of Small Businesses found that its members spend proportionally five times more than their larger rivals in complying with EU regulations. All this bodes ill for the culture of enterprise and competitiveness of European societies.

'You are knocking on an open door' responded Lydia. 'The Lisbon Strategy is designed to make Europe the most competitive economic space in the world. The Commission now focuses on simplifying and improving both existing and new regulation to reinforce their effectiveness. Each new legal initiative of a General Directorate is now accompanied by an impact assessment report, which is then reviewed by an independent impact assessment board composed of the Deputy Secretary-General and four Directors-General. The deliberations of the board are made public. The European Commission has understood that less is more. The amount of legislation coming out of Brussels has been reduced substantially, making scrutiny by the European Parliament and national parliaments that much easier. I have reason to believe that the Commission is becoming more flexible, leaving ample room for exceptions to accommodate national sensitivities.'

But the cure proposed by the EC is itself a symptom of disease. The current response to anxieties is to propose not less regulation but 'better' regulation: in other words, more of the same, but improved marketing. The 'Better Regulation Initiative', launched in 2004, has involved repealing only those regulations which have become 'irrelevant or obsolete' – for example, an obscure Directive from the 1960s on measuring the size of knots in wood. The main thrust of the EU's efforts lies in a three-year programme to 'codify' existing regulation, so as to reduce its 'volume', in the way that printing on India paper reduces the volume of a bible. Meanwhile, only 0.5% of EU regulations are subject to assessment for their economic impact, and there is no clear obligation on those who frame the regulations to take note of criticisms. Scrutiny committees in national parliaments have neither the time nor the expertise to deal with the flood of proposals from Brussels; nor do they have the motive to take action. They know that their objections can be effective only if backed by the full weight of their government with the Commission.

Among the regulations now in force are some of such palpable absurdity that they would not survive for a moment if there were any means to remove them. But that is precisely the problem: nothing in Europe ever goes into reverse. So we are saddled with the EU Directive for Personal Protective Equipment 89/696, which requires Wellington boots to be sold with a 24-page user's manual in 10 languages, giving advice on risk assessment, storage conditions, life expectancy, washing in a mild detergent, and resistance to electricity, cold weather and oil (though not water). Users are advised to try each boot for fitting before use, and even the amount of energy absorbed by the heels is recorded. The manufacturers are required to test their boots twice a month at EU approved laboratories to ensure that they comply with standards. And so on. Equally absurd is the draft Directive on ladders, which insists that 'ladders shall be so positioned as to ensure their stability during use', and which tells us that 'the holding of the ladder by another person as a safety measure shall not be allowed'.

An essential source of over-regulation in Europe is the peculiar legislative structure of the EU, which, although it issues its 'legal instruments' from the Council of Ministers, has no real legislative assembly. Its deliberations are supposedly subject to counter-balancing influence from the Permanent Representatives of the Member States, meeting as 'COREPER'. But these Permanent Representatives are, by virtue of their permanence, entrenched bureaucrats of the same complexion as those they are appointed to influence. Their relation to public opinion or real interests in the nation state that they represent is entirely uncertain, given that no election can ever remove them from office. It is true that, under the 'co-decision' procedure, the European Parliament has a 'staying order' over legislative decisions, and can send back its objections to the Council, indicating what changes it would accept. However, the Parliament is not the originator of legislation, and has so little legitimacy in the eyes of the European electorates that it is seen more as a lobbying machine than as a legislature. Lydia, I should say, is a passionate defender of the European Parliament, believing that many of the existing problems can be solved by expanding its powers. But it seems to me that the Council is not going to relinquish its powers to such a ramshackle institution, and that in any case the Parliament will never be able to exercise them in a coherent way, composed as it is of members so diverse in culture, language and political tradition.

Not that the Council is very much better placed to make rational decisions. It consists of people far too busy to examine the documents put before them and records of its decisions are made available only after measures have been agreed. Most often, package deals tie together non-related regulation as a result of long-winded bargaining. The legal instruments themselves, whether in the form of regulations, decisions or Directives, are prepared by a busy army of bureaucrats within the European Commission, rather than by elected representatives of the people. These bureaucrats suffer no penalty for their mistakes, are unknown to the people and cannot be removed from office by those whom their decisions affect. Their business is to regulate. If ever it were decided that no more regulations are needed, there would be no further use for them, except to police the surviving edicts. Hence, following the logic of Parkinson's Law – as confirmed by the Public Choice theory of rent-seeking* – the bureaucrats of

---

* The Public Choice theory of Rent-Seeking, as elaborated by James Buchanan and Gordon Tulloch, explains how individuals may receive political rents in the form of access to public money by virtue not of what they do or what they own but solely by virtue of who they are within the structures of power over the masses. Thomas Jefferson warned of this danger, to which Publia draws attention in the behaviour of functionaries of the European Union, a few years before the writing of *The Federalist Papers*, as follows: 'The public money and public liberty ... will soon be discovered to be sources of wealth and dominion to those who hold them; distinguished, too, by this tempting circumstance, that they are the instrument, as well as the object of acquisition. With money we will get men, said Caesar, and with men we will get money.' Thomas Jefferson, *Notes on Virginia*, 1784

the Commission seek to expand the reach and number of their products, their staff and armies of experts. One of the less obvious causes for overregulation identified by seasoned observers is the tendency of national politicians to use the European level as a way of introducing legislation that could not find supporters at home. Another overlooked cause is continuous enlarging of EU legislative competency by the European Court of Justice.

Many matters fundamental to the identity of the local and national cultures of Europe have already been subjected to central regulation, and the legislative machine is such that scrutiny by national parliaments may be entirely ineffective to stem the flow. Thus, for example, Latvia's once thriving sugar industry is no more. Sugar production quotas stipulated by the EU, together with heavy fines imposed on Latvia for storing 'unusual' amounts of produce before EU accession, brought about its demise. The loss was accepted as a price of gaining EU membership for a country that joined the EU with both hope and despair. In a similar manner, 'health and safety' measures have been used to destroy local markets, while Directive 92/46/EEC, regulating the production and marketing of raw milk, heat-treated milk and milk-based products is putting the small cheese-makers of France out of business. Likewise, the small farmers of Romania will no longer be able to sell their produce at the farm gate, since EU regulations insist on the packaging of agricultural products. This one regulation, if followed to the letter, will mean the end of traditional Romanian agriculture, and the surrender of that still beautiful countryside to agribusiness – a sad reward for the peasant farmers who were the backbone of their country and the target of Ceaucescu's insane and vindictive modernism.

As a rejoinder, Lydia enumerated a long list of regulation-based economic benefits, such as lower airfares and cheaper textile imports. She reminded me that whenever you abolish frontiers, new functions tend to develop. 'All of a sudden, issues firmly in the national realm can take on a European dimension, for example in the area of the environment, where climate change is forcing countries to adopt common measures. For example, the fear of terrorist attacks on the occasion of Crown Prince Frederik's wedding in 2004 helped overcome Danish resistance to cooperation in the area of "Justice and Home Affairs".'

I am well aware of the many benefits, most of them not in question. What preoccupies me is the price we pay in distortion and compliance. Take lobbying. A member of an elected national assembly will respond to lobbying from interest groups and businesses: but his response will be noticed by the electorate and could jeopardize his position. In a normal legislature, therefore, lobbying has an effect only on the margins of legislation, and is always an object of suspicion to the ordinary voter. Not so the lobbying in Brussels. For lobbying is the only outside pressure that the bureaucrats feel and its rewards are enormous. A manufacturer of specialized car-seats for children, who can secure a regulation imposing such seats by law, does not merely steal a competitive advantage in one country. If the law is issued by Brussels, it gives him a competitive advantage in 27 countries. And the example illustrates the way in which competitive advantage can be pursued under the guise of 'health and safety'. For the very reason that the legislative powers of the Commission can address any issue that affects the single market, private interest groups can masquerade as public spirited lobbyists. Increasingly, firms lobby for regulations that tie the hands of the competition, rather than regulations that ensure a 'level playing field', and this negative approach operates at the level of national governments as well as individual businesses.

However, the effect of regulation is by no means uniform across the Union. We should take note of this, since it shows how the effort to unify the continent through edicts amplifies the real and enduring diversity of its cultures. Unlike EU 'regulations',

which are directly applicable in the Member States without further action from the authorities, EU 'Directives' leave the governments of Member States free to choose the form and method
whereby their objectives might be realized. While both are binding, Directives will be interpreted differently across the Union.
They tend to be strictly interpreted in Britain, Germany, Scan-
dinavia and Holland, and enforced through the law, but treated
more leniently and enforced with less severity in Spain and Italy.
In France they are often strictly interpreted but ignored. For
example, France is currently being pursued for its failure to con-
form properly or even at all with Directives on Genetically Modified Organisms, nitrate levels in water and dumping of waste
in landfill sites. And the pursuit is largely pointless, since the EU
commands no sanctions (short of the ultimate, and therefore
unusable, sanction of expulsion) with which to bring recalcitrant
members into line. More often than not, Member States pay the
fines and continue violating the rules.

These differences are not accidental. On the contrary, they
reflect deep cultural differences, both in the attitude to law and
in the attitude to political authority. The Dutch, the Scandina-
vians, the Germans and the British have an innate respect for
law that derives in part from their cultural inheritance, in part
from the procedures followed by their courts. The top-down
approach of Napoleonic legislation and legal procedure means
that law, for the French, is the tool of government, whose edicts
are to be evaded wherever possible. And in eastern Europe,
after 50 years in which the courts were mere instruments of
social control, in which civil law was virtually non-existent,
and where the gap between accusation and punishment was
filled by a rubber stamp, the people look on law with a quizzical
and ironical attitude. Law, in their experience, has nothing to
do with justice. Under communism, laws were shorthand for
arbitrary punishments, which could be avoided only by clan-

destine deals enforced without the help of the State. The current transitional period is inevitably riddled with black markets and insidious involvement in the regular economy of former employees of the system. To this day, therefore, vast tracts of the East European economies remain unregulated, with black market networks still intact.

I felt that Lydia was beginning to lose patience with my critique. She rounded on me for my failing to realize that an internal market of 27 required substantial regulation at EU level. There is not much of our lives unlinked to the economy, so a vast, interventionist body of law was absolutely essential. As a matter of fact, the *acquis* mirrored faithfully the complexities of our modern life. She took the trouble to explain that you have to differentiate between three types of regulations: competition enabling regulation (setting common rules in order to create a competitive internal market), competition sustaining regulation (fighting against illegal subsidies and support) and a third type that falls neither into the first, nor the second category, whose necessity can and should be debated. She was scathing about people who wielded the word 'regulation' as a club to hammer the Commission, when in reality it stood for economic development, the protection of the consumer, of health and the environment, of cultural diversity – the cogent interests of the common good.

Whilst Lydia followed her aspirational instincts, I was looking at some hard facts. In all its forms, regulation has a dangerous tendency to ignore the law of unintended consequences. The solution to one problem may be the start of another. In an elected and accountable legislature, with open and transparent committees and full scrutiny by the press, voices from beyond the chamber can point out the undesirable side-effects of legislation. This does not happen, however, when regulations are conceived by bureaucrats. Two far-reaching examples will illustrate what I mean. Since 1996, the EU has issued a series of Directives on air quality, limiting the size and quantity of dust particles in the air. These Directives, passed into Dutch law in 2001, require concentrations of dust that could not be achieved in a densely populated country like Holland, where in any case sea salt and soil clouds constitute 55% of the atmospheric dust content, and two-thirds of the remainder is blown in from abroad. Nevertheless, the law has been enforced, bringing a large number of building projects to an end, including roads, industrial parks and housing projects in the centre of Amsterdam, since the ambient dust surpassed permitted EU levels. Epidemiological studies indicate that, thanks to atmospheric dust, the lifespan of some thousands of people is reduced by a few days to a few months. Nevertheless, the Environment Commissioner insists on yet more stringent regulations, to be put in place in 2010 and 2015, arguing that delays in reaching the chosen targets 'would be playing with people's lives'. That it might be playing rather more seriously with people's lives by failing to provide the housing required to shelter them or the industry required to employ them is not a relevant consideration: for those things belong to another department, and the essence of bureaucratic regulation is that it proceeds problem by problem and neither needs, nor is able, to take account of the whole.

The second case concerns a European Directive issued in response to the slight risk that diseased animals might enter the human food-chain. It insists that all slaughter should now take place in the presence of a qualified vet, who must inspect each animal as it arrives at the abattoir. There is no evidence that veterinary examination in these circumstances is either necessary or (in the rare cases when infected animals come to the abattoir) effective. Nevertheless, the Directive was issued, and passed into British law. The effect of this on husbandry, on farming communities and the viability of small pasture farms has been devastating. Now, elected politicians, in need of the goodwill of their constituents, would have taken into account not only the small risk addressed by such a Directive, but also the huge risks posed to the farming community by the destruction of local abattoirs, the avoidable stress posed to animals by long journeys, the benefits of localized food production and local markets for meat, and so on. As rational beings, they would recognize that risks don't come in atomic particles, but are parts of complex organisms, shaped by the flow of events. And they would know in their hearts that there is no more risky practice than that of disaggregating risks, so as one by one to forbid them. Even bureaucrats, in their own private lives, will take the same line. They too are rational beings, and know that risks must be constantly taken, and constantly weighed against each other. However, when bureaucrats legislate for others, and suffer no cost should they get things wrong, they will inevitably look for a single and specific problem, and seize on a single and absolute principle in order to solve it.

All modern economies are subject to regulation both from within, by increasingly statist legislatures, and from without, by international norms set by international bodies like the UN and its agencies and the WTO. What is unusual in the EU machine is, first, the existence of an all-authorizing project, which enables legislators to invade territory after territory, recognizing none as lying outside their writ and, secondly, the lack of real accountability for mistakes, or of real pressure to rectify them.

It seems to me that there is no alternative now but to return the primary legislative responsibility to national legislatures. Parliaments should set the limits on how far governments could bind them through the European treaties. Only with such a mandate would the Council of Ministers have power to issue a regulation as a legal instrument. The right to initiate regulations should be vested in the national assemblies themselves, and

neither the Commission nor the Council of Ministers should
have independent legislative powers. It should be possible to test
regulations through pilot schemes and to guarantee their future
extinction through sunset clauses should they prove ineffective
or unworkable. In short, we should return to the regulatory
process those safeguards that reason itself recommends.

The first effect of such reforms would be to slow down the
rate at which new regulations are introduced – at first to near
zero, surely a welcome result, and one that would enable Europe
to take a much needed breath. The second effect would be to
enable national parliaments to decide which aspects of their
national life are open to regulation on 'Single Market' principles, and which are not. The third effect would be to restore
the legal authority of regulations, which would be reconnected
to the democratic process, and to those who could be held to
account for agreeing to them. Regulation would cease to be
the alien and alienating thing that it has become, and re-assume
something of the character of law.

When I presented my ideas to Lydia, she made an interesting observation. 'You acknowledge', she said, 'the need for
Union-wide regulation, and the need to ensure that regulations
are not just enforceable but also reversible. Who could disagree with that? But you seem to think that you will achieve that
result by repatriating regulatory powers. Is there any evidence
that national legislatures will do a better job than the Commission? Look at any economy outside the European Union – that
of the United States, for example – and you will find the same
accumulation of dead or dying regulations, the same motive
to evade their force, and the same inertia when it comes to
removing or revising them. And the United States is the best of
the bunch. Elsewhere, regulation has got to the point where it
is impossible to comply with it. In South America, it is virtually impossible legally to launch a business. Why assume that it

will be any different in Europe? Rather than adopt your radical proposals, we should tackle failure of the European institutions to define which matters can be regulated centrally. And this is a matter for collective decision by the European Union as a whole. Leave it to the Member States and the old rivalries will immediately prevail, destroying all that we have gained by way of a single market. It functions best with a strong Commission President, someone with credibility inside the system and who is knowledgeable, like Jacques Delors. Such a person would be able to reconcile factions inside the European Commission. But, contrary to popular myth, we do not deal with advocates of a Soviet-style planned economy. The estimate of the frighteningly high number of national regulations supposedly originating in Brussels – repeatedly reported in the press as 80% – is populist and totally unfounded. A 2006 assessment of German federal law revealed that concentration of EU regulation was highest in the area of environmental protection where it reached 81%, which makes perfect sense given its technical and cross-border nature. It is much lower in other areas, for example 15% in labour and social policy, and around 40% in the area of finance and economics.

European institutions have by and large understood that it is important to give leeway to the nation states, to allow for flexibility and to respect national sensitivities. The idea of harmonization is just one instrument. Others increasingly widely used are convergence and mutual recognition, as well as effective cooperation between administrations, be it at national or EU level. This is a novel mixture to deal with a novel circumstance. It is why it was perfectly correct of the EU Commission President Barroso to describe the EU as a new political entity, a non-imperial empire – the first to be constructed with full consent.'

'My dear Lydia,' I replied, 'history is against you. All empires rest on centralized power and force.'

Reversibility

You don't have to be what my English friends call a 'Eurosceptic' to believe that the acquis communautaire lies at the heart of the project of European integration. The term denotes the entire body of laws, policies and practices which have at any given time evolved within the EC and the EU; but, as its name implies, it refers especially to those laws and procedures in which the central apparatus has acquired powers previously exercised by the Member States. Only with the Maastricht Treaty of 1992 did the term become part of the official terminology. But some years before then, it had become clear that the acquis is in fact the real and lasting achievement of the Union. It obliges Member States to accept all previous and future centralizing measures, while implicitly ruling out the repatriation of any powers lost. The written laws, regulations and procedures of the acquis now amount to over 170,000 pages. Few experts have knowledge of much more than a tiny part. To go from page to page is to receive an impression of meddlesomeness verging on the surreal. This impression is as common among believers in the project of 'ever closer union' as it is among the advocates of real subsidiarity. Everyone seems to agree that something has gone wrong; that a machine has been put in place that lacks some of the gears necessary to reverse or moderate speed. Thus it has one of the in-built flaws of one party states – the total lack of will and ability to respond to valid criticism from anyone outside the charmed leadership circle. The tragic consequences of this are a matter for history.

As I outlined my thoughts, Lydia's frown became severe. What she said reflected her mood: 'Let me deal head-on with one of the darkest charges that people of your persuasion often level at the supporters of integration. It is that, in some way, those of us who are building Europe's future seek by covert means to make the project of the new Europe irreversible. I plead guilty to the charge. It is true that we seek to make the reality of Europe that we have achieved so far irreversible. Of course we do. In order not to let slip the important gains we have achieved, we need to build a reality that is both practical and cultural. So we had to pursue a particular path, which may be oblique, but I am more than happy to defend its rationale in open debate.

Ours is a task that is noble and unusual in the long history of the European peoples. Once the constitution, now called the 'Lisbon Treaty', is ratified in 2008, it will change centuries of history. This is an outcome that is entirely beneficial. The moral case for having introduced irreversibility into the legislative and treaty processes of Europe derives directly from the reasons why our project has been undertaken. For, make no mistake, we seek here permanently to discipline and limit the powers of the individual nations. They have caused too much grief in the past. Thus, it is a vital attribute of the construction that powers – what in the Union are called 'competencies' – are never to be reclaimed. Otherwise, we would risk losing that which has been so painfully gained. I wish that those proposing the ever-wider embrace of European regulation would candidly admit this, for it does our cause no disservice, nor does it weaken our case.

The more practical justifications for irreversibility are manifold. Regulations are the result of a set of complex negotiations that always involve compromises on matters not germane to the specific regulation in question. To undo a package deal may have ramifications. Like a hidden thread, once you unpick it, you never know how far the entire construction will unravel. If regulation is stable and secure, businesses are able to plan for the long-term based on the expectation of an emerging and developing pan-European environment for trade and manufacturing. They will be secure in the knowledge that all the measures in support of economic activity in the social sphere will remain in place or even widen their scope, but, certainly, never be retrenched.

However, the case for insisting on irreversibility is even more compelling in the cultural domain. As Jean Monnet understood clearly at the outset, the task of building a new Europe is one that must pass through several human generations. It must, in that process, condition the public mind in its expectations and help to relegate the memory of Europe's painful past to the history books. That is, of course, the rationale for the principle of ever closer union in the Treaty of Rome and for the need for the ECJ to outrank national supreme courts. Irreversibility is both logical and reasonable.'

Lydia's candour left me momentarily speechless. But I was quick then to congratulate her on it, both as a sign of our friendship and as valuable in our exchange; for it licensed me to respond in like measure. I replied thus:

'In his letters to the American people, Publius makes it clear that the worst kind of government is not that which makes mistakes but that which, while making mistakes, is *unable to correct them*. When the powers of government are properly divided, and when those with sovereignty can be ejected by a vote, mistakes may be remedied. But suppose the institutions of government are set up in such a way that all concentration of power is irreversible, so that powers acquired by the centre can never be recaptured? And suppose that those who rule at the centre are appointed, cannot be removed at popular request, meet in secret and keep few or no minutes of their decisions? Does anyone think that, in such circumstances, the conditions exist in which mistakes can be rectified, or even cogently admitted?

Any system having few, if any, ways of rectifying mistakes or of holding decision-makers accountable cannot endure; for it ends up friendless. The *acquis* is a sure proof of this. It is always growing, and no addition to it is ever lost. However foolish it may be for the European institutions to take charge of some matter best dealt with by the Member States, no power, once transferred, is ever recaptured. Ridiculous regulations can be duly laughed at from top to bottom of the Union; but the laughter rings hollow, since it meets with no response. A cavernous void lies at the heart of the European process, a void into which questions are constantly called out by the people and from which no answer ever returns. Reversibility has been marginalized *ab initio*. It seems to me that this failing is a structural failing, and one that cannot be remedied without radical reform. But there are signs of how that forlorn state may be avoided, and they are to be found in surprising places. One is the political settlement that preceded the introduction of the euro.

Since Member States were allowed from the outset to 'opt out', leaving the eurozone is not tantamount to breaking with the Union. If, for example, Italy were forced to go back to the Lira, an eventuality by no means outside the realm of possibilities, she would still remain a full member just like Britain, Sweden, Denmark and the other 12 countries with their own currencies. So, reversibility simply does not have the apocalyptic tinge that you give it.

But this exception, although highly significant, merely proves the rule. For the most part, once a power is transferred to the European Union, there is no place left to which a Member State can return. A place outside the Common Agricultural Policy, for example, is *ipso facto* a place outside the Treaties, and therefore a place outside the Union. It is this that makes it so difficult for Member States to renegotiate any detail of the Union's legislation, however damaging to its own interest that detail may be. The response is always the nuclear one: either you're in the Union, or you're out of it. Periodic promises by British and Danish politicians to renegotiate the Common Fisheries Policy, for example, ring hollow: no procedure exists for accomplishing such a goal – all that can be done is to utter vacuous threats to leave the Union, followed by a grumbling acquiescence in the *status quo*.

This irreversible quality attaches also to the laws and regulations of the Union. Laws which, once accepted, become subsumed under a treaty are laws of a radically different status from laws passed by a normal legislative assembly. When a national assembly passes a bad law, a subsequent assembly can repeal it: no procedure is required to undo the mistake other than the one that first produced it. But the peculiar nature of European law forbids this simple process of rectification. Law, once made, is taken out of the sphere of discussion and insulated from repeal by its status under the Treaties. Since no Member State will contemplate repudiating the Treaties, at any rate for so simple a matter as an irksome regulation or even a large but bearable financial cost, bad laws remain on the books, buried in the countless pages of the *acquis communautaire*. These laws, by tying the hands of the European states, are making Europe as a whole increasingly less competitive in the world economy. In terms of statistics, with notable variation between national economies, our continent is on the slide in the global league table. There are, of course, other factors that reinforce this alarming trend, but the EU regulatory structure makes its own unwelcome contribution.

Perhaps the most damaging aspect of bad or questionable laws, however, is that they are bringing the entire legislative process into disrepute. Each piece of European legislation creates a minor national industry, devoted to interpreting, elaborating and enforcing the Brussels hand-down. The Health and Safety regulations breed a range of inspectorates, all looking for work, all building their own expanding empires. The same applies in all spheres of EU activities. So any flaw in the abstract original is magnified in the practical application of the rule on the ground. The reaction to senseless regulation varies widely across the continent. Some nations tend to grumble and obey; others build secret resentments; many find ways round it and yet others simply ignore it. Eventually, however, the habit of disobedience will become so widespread that the people of Europe will consider themselves as little bound to obey the European Commission as the Commission feels bound to account to the people.'

As I said this, a wry smile played across Lydia's lips, as if she was sorry for someone who lacked vision and could not muster enough imagination to visualize a glorious future emerging from the sad shambles of today. 'It is so typical of the small-minded to seize only on the negatives, to carp endlessly on deficiencies, to dwell on what does not work and ignore the promise of what is to come. Even if we admit the shortcomings you love to highlight, and there is obviously a lot in what you claim, we prefer to look at the bigger picture and take a more balanced view.

Why is it that when tackling the question of reversibility it is exclusively discussed in terms of powers to be taken from the European level to be exercised nationally? The question of what could best be done at the European instead of at the national level is neglected, as if somehow Europe is tainted. Actually, there have been serious attempts to explore 'repatriation'. They have not been successful, because in our current structure, given the Single Market, to repatriate powers is impossible. Whereas qualified majority can move powers to the centre, to reverse it takes unanimity.

If you are really serious about checks and balances, as our American friends call it, the remedy lies at the European level. Surely the European Parliament is the only body to provide them? At the moment it is rather feeble and has precious few powers. But it is bound to grow in stature, in authority, in effectiveness as we construct the federal state. Eventually, once elected by a single electorate right across the continent, it will have the same legitimacy as any of any of its national counterparts. Some of my friends even visualize that the national parliaments will by then resemble regional assemblies, like the organs of the Länder in Germany or the Scottish Parliament, while the decisive democratic centre of gravity will reside at the heart of Europe. In the meantime, we have to suffer the administration we have, irreversibility and all. The price is well worth paying.'

I refuse these terms of debate. For me, it is better to think of an alternative now that will restore to the European nations the kind of government that can rectify its own mistakes. But how do we secure reversibility in agreements between sovereign states? If the only way of reversing anything is to repudiate the original treaty, all alternatives to the EU will suffer from the defect that I have been describing.

The answer, surely, is to design new treaties *in which reversibility is part of the deal*. This would entail a less rigid approach. Perhaps regulations should be of two kinds. First, those to provide a firm foundation with rules necessary to the operation of the Single Market. These rules should be kept to the minimum necessary to achieve the goal, and should be the subject of unanimous agreement, with every Member State retaining a veto against their adoption. Secondly, there should be a further set of regulations which remain optional – and these a Member State could opt to join if it is in its interest to do so, and also to leave when that seems advisable. National legislatures could have the final say in adopting or refusing regulations of this second kind, and also the first say in proposing them. The Commission itself would then coordinate rather than impose or revoke such rules. Once adopted, however, rules and regulations of both kinds would fall under the jurisdiction of the European Court of Justice, which, re-tasked, should be strictly bound to judge any dispute in accordance with the rules that apply to it, and would have no power to improvise according to some transcendental goal of 'ever closer union'. Instead, the Court's guiding light would be a reality in which diversity is as estimable as unity. The 'construction' of the last 50 years will be superseded.

Lydia flashed back: 'An idea to destroy all that has been achieved! It might be wondered whether, in such circumstances, any Member State would really "opt in" to any aspect of the treaty that involved a transfer of sovereign powers.'

'No,' I replied, 'I disagree. It seems to me that opting in, when made safe by the possibility of opting out, would occur quite frequently. And it would introduce a refreshing aspect of experiment and competition into the European Institutions. States with similar systems of criminal law – France, Italy and Spain, for instance – could opt in to a shared jurisdiction, with cross-frontier policing and criminal trials. Others might opt in to joint command structures for their military, or joint environmental policies. The resulting union would be maximally diverse, but still something more than a collection of bilateral

treaties. That is a credible way, which can retain the public support that Publius so correctly stressed as indispensable.'

Lydia looked deeply sceptical.

LETTER 10

Foreign Policy

Lydia and I have similar anxieties as we look ahead into the 21st century. Circumstances are not propitious for global security. The industrialization of China, with all the economic benefits it brings to the global consumer, comes at a very high price. It puts huge and rapidly increasing demands on the world's natural resources. The resulting pollution of the water, air and living environment of billions of Chinese may unleash a similar political upheaval to that which preceded the break-up of the Soviet system. Closer to home, we see the rise of Russia again, this time wearing not communist but nationalist clothes. Proud and bitter, reinforced by economic power based on mineral, oil and gas wealth, she is becoming a massive neighbour not inherently friendly towards us. This is aggravated by the absorption into the European Union of countries formerly under the heel of the Soviet regime. From across the Mediterranean, mass migration tells of failing states and poverty. And then we are confronted by a self-sacrificing, fanatical type of terrorism, drawing strength from one of the few, still expanding, major old religions. Add a fraying international system and strained alliances and the picture is indeed bleak.

Lydia has distinct ideas when it comes to confronting the dangers that lie ahead: 'We absolutely have to prepare for the trying times ahead. Facing a perilous world, European foreign policy would be much stronger united than a motley combination of single national policies could ever be. The Americans express this simple truth on their currency: *e pluribus unum*. Surely, if it is good for them, it is all the more vital for us in the old world who have only so recently resolved our own internal strife? But to be united, we need a wisely formulated EU foreign policy with a distinct voice. This will require sacrifices from countries like France and Great Britain who, as major powers, have for centuries geared their foreign policies to their national interests. But the gain for smaller nations, and for the continent as a whole, makes such sacrifice worthwhile. I am so happy to see the unity of purpose in the Constitutional Reform Treaty that paves the way for a European Foreign Service, soon to be followed by the establishment of embassies of the Union across the world. The foreign minister, so called or not, would be respected as the authentic voice of Europeans henceforth.

No-one believes that such transitions of power are easy. This is why, as throughout the forging of the EU, we must advance by creating permanent institutions and move carefully, step by measured step, in the way that an experienced mountaineer climbs a mountain. Each institution is a piton into the rock face that gives both security and the opportunity to climb yet higher. I therefore fully agree with the Commissioner for External Affairs, when she says that Europe should aim to have a seat on the UN Security Council. The time when Britain and France best defended the interests of their countries on their own is long past. These are simply anachronisms from the age of violence that we have left. Incidentally, the abolishing of one of the European seats enables finally the reform of membership of the Security Council, often attempted and never realized. Therefore, Europe has the opportunity not only to give greater weight to its foreign policy in these councils where this matters, but also to make the single most important contribution that might help reanimate that other great multilateral creation of the mid-20th century, the United Nations itself.

A further reason for supporting the move towards a common European foreign policy, now that such a great instrument has been incorporated in the Lisbon Treaty, is Europe's strength in soft power. The ability of Europeans to negotiate, to mediate, to find reasonable compromise amongst ourselves, which has been one of the most reassuring successes in the very creation of the Union, is also an object lesson to a fractious and dangerous world. We are a pool of peace in a world of much violence and, unlike the United States, we have a highly attractive model for the future development of other regions of the world. It is a Union model, which we can export. This is a valuable asset that should be at the heart of our foreign policy.

For the European Union is, after all, as President Barroso of the Commission has wisely observed, a strange beast. It is a new form – a genuinely new form – of political entity. It is the first non-imperial imperial power in which there has been a voluntary and happy surrender of sovereignties for the greater good of all. That the Union has now achieved the status of a single legal entity, permitting it to sign treaties, is the culmination of a hope engendered in the original Treaty. With the various institutional organs of our foreign policy in place, Europeans could contribute to the next stage of world civilization in ways as powerful as but more humane than those which Europe gave during the age of imperial expansion. It is a mission which can rightly enthuse the younger generation of Europeans as they experience the pride of being part of a civilized identity. It is a mission to share peace and prosperity with the wider human community.

According to many opinion polls, the emergence of a fully fledged foreign policy of the European Union is eagerly awaited by European citizens. It will share the great benefits of the European model globally. The EU is an international public good. Over the years, we have developed unique comprehensive crisis management capabilities to tackle what one could call the 'dark side of globalization': economic turbulence, demographic movements, climate change and economic development. We are able to make peace, train police forces and judges, foster economic development and make sure human rights are guarded. Our approach ably combines the soft power of the Commission with the hard power of the Member States – soft power with hard edges. We will have to invest in hard power capabilities, not in order to compete with anybody else but in order to be able to react quickly in times of emergency and to be credible.

Regrettably but unavoidably, our foreign policy will have to contain certain elements of *Realpolitik*. It is vital for the survival of Europe to develop joint strategic visions on major foreign policy challenges. After taking an extended holiday from history, we are now finding out what a messy place the world still is.

It is true that currently we have quite a range of national foreign policy positions. Not all 27 countries will be able to influence specific foreign policy decisions. But I firmly believe that, through osmosis and maybe helped along by crisis, we will reach common view points.'

I cannot say I am surprised by Lydia's sincerely held beliefs. Many people among my acquaintances, who are architects and builders of the Greater Europe project, think likewise. For myself, I am convinced that such beliefs are not only misguided, but are actually harmful.

The European Union itself is the product of independent foreign policies of nation states. It is not the policy of one state

only. All its institutions and procedures have been created by
agreement between the Member States exercising their sovereign powers. The new extensions to the now so-called Lisbon
Treaty demand that the EU has a foreign policy of its own, with a
foreign minister, presumably with a fully equipped department
to implement it. But this presupposes that Member States have
bought into the foreign policy as exercised by the foreign minister representing the voice of Europe. What is the likelihood
of that? It depends on how closely they are associated with the
line taken by the EU, and how far it accords with their national
interest. Judging by the brief history of the Union so far, these
interests seldom converge. How can they? France is nearly self-
sufficient in energy, Germany is badly dependent on Russian
supplies; the Baltic countries and Poland are at the front line
of confrontation with Russian imperialism, Portugal and Spain
are distant from it; Britain is wedded to NATO, France sees
herself at the heart of an emerging European-centred military
alliance. In the recent past, the nations of Europe were divided
on policy directed at the Balkan crisis, on action over Iraq, on
the supply of armaments to the Third World, on the reform of
the United Nations and just about on anything of international
importance when more than words were involved. Lisbon has
hosted a great Afro-European summit from which Britain, the
largest single donor to Africa with the most extensive relations
in that continent, was forced to exclude itself by the presence
of President Mugabe who, single-handedly, destroyed the very
livelihood of his own country.

The question then is what difference a European foreign
minister could make? Would he spend his time criss-crossing
the continent trying to broker deals among 27 members, as
some sort of compromise not quite to the satisfaction of any
one of them? Or would he undertake to re-educate the Member
States on their national interests? Or would he manufacture his

own policies and try to impose them on 27 more or less reluctant national ministers? Would these policies be outlined whilst being finalized or emerge during EU negotiations with third parties? Would an EU foreign minister ever be in a position to guarantee delivery of the terms of EU signed agreements whilst they had to be provided by the nation states? If not, what credibility would such an EU foreign minister have with our friends, or enemies and global institutions? On the face of it, such a peripatetic minister would not make much of a difference. It is the absence of European solidarity and common purpose that is missing, not a European minister. Any common foreign policy must come before an institution to house it otherwise the institution would be as hollow as the European Parliament building in Strasbourg.

In this context, our conversation veered naturally to the USA. 'As you know,' Lydia said, 'I dislike the anti-Americanism traditionally prevalent in Europe. Over the years, I have come round to America as one of the apostles of Enlightenment doing her best to export her vision across the globe. But Europe too is an apostle of Enlightenment; and the European vision is distinct from the American. And in the world as it is today, when America is not only the sole superpower but also an object of far-reaching and even implacable hostility around the world, it is vital that Europe acquire an identity of its own, and not be tarred with the brush of American policy, for example in its intervention in Iraq. Because we have no foreign policy of our own, the world does not know what we stand for and therefore assumes, since there is no real evidence to the contrary, that we stand for America.'

I could not deny the force of Lydia's argument. It is clear that the American approach to foreign policy is very different from the approach historically taken by the European states; the Iraq war being clear proof of this. Seemingly indifferent to the artificial nature of Iraq, to its lack of a cohesive identity, to the bitter conflicts that divide Sunni from Shi'ite and Arab from Kurd, the Americans tried to create a democratic nation state in a place where no cohesive nation existed and democracy was unknown. The naivety of this is perhaps more apparent in retrospect than it was at the time. But no official of the Quai d'Orsay would have recommended this kind of 'regime change' because the long experience of dealing with Muslims in North Africa and the Middle East has convinced the French that nothing is more likely to unite the Muslims against us than the attempt to impose democratic citizenship, in which religion is privatized and toleration compelled.

However, I could not help thinking that the example did nothing to support Lydia's case. Faced with the crisis in Iraq, the nation states of Europe divided along the historical fault-lines that have always appeared in emergencies. The Quai d'Orsay reacted in the spirit of Louis Massignon, a French scholar on Islam, deploring this clumsy intervention in a region that only long experience, linguistic competence and cross-cultural flair could open to outside understanding. The British followed the Americans into the breach, aware of their historical obligations as the original creators of Iraq. The Poles, the Czechs and the Slovaks too joined in, not out of 'Europeanism', but in order to demonstrate to the Americans that they are now trustworthy military partners, and loyal members of the Alliance on which they might at any moment depend, should Russia flex its muscles. The Spaniards joined in hesitantly, unsure of their interest in doing so, and immediately withdrew when terrorist bombings in Madrid alerted them to the danger of meddling in the Muslim world. Each nation, in short, pursued its own perceived interests, in ways that were more or less consistent with the past flow of foreign policy. Had there been, at the time, a European foreign ministry, charged with creating a policy common to the nation states of Europe, what policy could it conceivably have come up with? If a policy of non-intervention, would the ministry have imposed this on the British, the Dutch, the Danes, the Spaniards, the Czechs, the Slovaks and the Poles, forcing them to choose between the Atlantic Alliance and Europe? If a policy of war alongside the United States, would it have imposed this on the French, forcing them to abandon their posture as the impartial protector of the Muslims, or on the Germans, the Belgians or the Greeks? Of course, neither course of action would have been practical, and in any case each of them would have led to such intractable protests and negotiations that nothing would have been resolved until the moment for action had passed.

But I agree with Lydia that the anti-American feeling in Europe cannot be ignored. Whether we share it or deplore it, it is a hue that tints any thoughts on the future of our continent. The first thing to note is that this shift of sentiment demonstrates how far European politics have changed since the days of the Treaty of Rome. In the 1950s, the prevailing mood was one of gratitude to the USA for saving the continent from fascism and afterwards for fortifying it against Soviet subversion through the Marshall Plan. However, it is a law of human nature that gratitude gives way to resentment, as the image of one's dependence grows. This resentment has been amplified by the growing influence of American popular culture, a culture which is unpopular to the more subtle European taste.

The more I reflect on such facts, however, the more it seems to me that foreign policy is not and cannot be the business of the European Union. The existence of the Union creates new interests. It changes fundamentally many of the short-term and long-term goals of national diplomacy; and it makes the 'special relationship' between Britain and America at times especially irksome to the rest of us. But it does not create the conditions for an independent foreign policy that could subsume the policies of the nation states. European solidarity is an input into national diplomacy; not the goal of it. That goal remains what it has always been, the national interest.

'How then', asked Lydia, 'do you prevent the large powers – who are, after all, the powers with which we most need to secure agreements – from playing off the nations of Europe against each other? How will the smaller European nations protect their national interests within the international arena, unless through a greater community? When the Italian and the German commercial delegations both present themselves at the Chinese foreign office, how do you prevent the Chinese from bargaining each of them down, by promising a deal with only one of them? And how do we manage the oil-rich, nuclear-armed and rampant Russia, if we must manage it state by state and without a common policy? Surely, in the world as it now is, the nation states will count for nothing if they cannot, in foreign relations, pool their sovereignty and their bargaining power.'

My response is simple. If the Chinese want to play off one European nation against another, in the natural process of competition whereby nations discover and develop their markets, a hypothetical common European foreign policy will not make any difference. The agreement between Russia and Germany for the supply of natural gas by pipeline was, on paper, an agreement to supply gas to Europe. But it contains no guarantee that at the end of the pipe-line on the Franco-German border there will still be some gas remaining. Nor does the agreement forbid the construction of the Baltic pipeline, which will leave the Russians with the power to cut off energy to Poland while still supplying Germany. This is the kind of national agreement that we must expect, with the 'European' component no better than window-dressing. For the Russians are like us – rational beings, who make agreements with sovereign entities and with long-term objectives in view. Why else is German ex-Chancellor Gerhard Schröder, in retirement, offered a position on the board of Gazprom? But Lydia elides two distinct categories in her pleas. Europe is part of, not the totality of, the 'West'.

Beyond mere economics, on a more profound level, the international interests of European states converge naturally in an entity loosely termed the 'West', the lynch pin of which is, of course, the Atlantic Alliance. The continued existence of this tried and trusted instrument *does* enable us to deal collectively with the Russian bear and could well help us with the Chinese dragon too. This does not mean that there is no need to coordinate European diplomacy. The French attitude that Europe's interests no longer coincide with those of the United States is widely shared among the Member States. With respect to the Middle East and Russia, the Europeans should coordinate their policies; recognizing the shared interest in opposing the global *jihad* of forces of radical Islamism against the West, and acknowledging the Russian longing to be fully included in a West, a 'West' centred on Europe, not America.

A second crucial distinction is also missing in Lydia's account. Coordinated policies are not shared policies. They have different sources, different principles of adaptation and different long-term goals. Only if we acknowledge this will we discover the path to a truly European future. For imagine what would happen if an EU foreign minister were actually appointed. Wandering the world with a portfolio of contradictory instructions; posturing as a single voice when he must change his tune from day to day; addressing every major issue with some stalling tactic while the 27 Member States strive to agree on their policy; and all the time trying to deceive the world into thinking that there is such a policy, and that it is a very good one except that he has temporarily forgotten it or mislaid the paper on which he once jotted it down. Acting thus, he will inflict the greatest damage on the perception of Europe in the wider world, and an equal damage on relations between the nation states that make up the Union.

LETTER 11

Security and Defence

The most basic relationship between any state and its citizen is one that guarantees individual freedom and security in return for obedience to the law and willingness to defend the state. Every state prefers to meet this obligation on its own but, over their history, few of them managed this feat without recourse to help from other states. The story of European wars is also the story of European alliances. Sometimes these alliances reached well beyond the boundaries of our continent. In fact, it was an alliance with America that saved democracy in Europe from dominant dictatorships of Right and Left three times in the last century. Thus far, all alliances have been limited in terms of time and objective, leaving the parties with their sovereignty intact. They have been coalitions of the willing, not the press-ganged. The European project is far more ambitious, because it recognizes no such limitations. In its ultimate logic, it seeks the fusion of defence and security, operating over and above the realm of nation states.

From the very beginning, the architects of European integration tried to create a European army. But in 1950, the idea

of a Europe-wide defence force came up against the obstacle
that nobody, not even the Germans, wished to see a properly
re-armed and militarily effective Germany. A compromise was
found with Germany joining the Western European Union in
1954 and NATO in 1955. That attempt to create a European
army was obviously premature, but, since Maastricht, matters
have moved apace.

We now have a 'Common Foreign and Security Policy',
boosted by a 'European Security Strategy', agreed by the Council
of Ministers in 2003. These initiatives have resulted in Europe-
wide military institutions, including a rapid reaction force,
battle groups, and a command structure that will permit joint
operations. A European Defence Agency to work on defence
capabilities development, research, acquisition and armament is
being generously funded by the Union (the 2008 budget totals
32 million euro, although the three-year budget has been vetoed
by the UK in November 2007). The Constitutional Treaty insists
that 'Member States shall actively and unreservedly support the
Union's common foreign and security policy in a spirit of loyalty and mutual solidarity.'* The provision in the Lisbon Treaty
alias the Constitution that 'The Union's competence in matters
of common foreign and security policy shall cover all areas of
foreign policy and all questions relating to the Union's security,
including the progressive framing of a common defence policy
that might lead to a common defence' is even more explicit.**

Lydia welcomes these developments and finds that the trend,
if anything, moves too slowly. I have grave reservations. The pro-
ponents of an integrated Europe, however, believed that a purely

---

* Part I, Title III 'Union Competences', Article I-16 The Common Foreign
and Security Policy, *Official Journal of the European Union*, 2004/C 310/01
** Title III, 'Provisions on the Institutions', Chapter 2 Specific Provisions
on the Common Foreign and Security Policy, Section 1, Art 11-1, *Official
Journal of the European Union*, 2007/C 306/01

European defence force would give external reality and internal focus to an emerging European entity. This belief led to the foundation of a Franco-German brigade in 1987, designed to incorporate German military potential while diluting German power. In 1993, the brigade was integrated into the Eurocorps composed of soldiers from Belgium, Luxembourg, Germany, France, and Spain under joint command following NATO's structures and procedures, to be put at the disposal of multinational organizations such as the UN, NATO or the EU. At the landmark Helsinki Summit in December 1999, Europeans stated that by 2003 the EU should be capable of deploying a 'European Rapid Reaction Force' (ERRF) of 60,000 troops. While most EU members want to balance their commitment to NATO and to the European Union, for others defence has become a political tool with which to advance the goal of European integration while undermining the North Atlantic Alliance, de-coupling Europe from America. Military effectiveness has taken second place to the ideal of a purely European defence potential – an ideal promised by French President Jacques Chirac in his speech to the NATO Riga Summit of 2006.

The distinction between political ambition and military common sense was highlighted at the 2000 Nice conference, from which delegates returned with conflicting beliefs about what had in fact been decided. The British believed that the proposed 'ERRF' would be controlled by the Deputy Supreme Allied Commander of NATO. In contrast, the view of Romano Prodi, then President of the Commission, was that the ERRF would be controlled by the European Union. In fact, the Nice Summit Decisions in the operational area of the European Security and Defence Policy (ESDP)* make it quite clear that

* See Treaty of Nice (*Official Journal* C 80 of 10 March 2001), Final Act, 1. Declaration on the European Security and Defence Policy, as well as Presidency Conclusions, Nice European Council Meeting, 7-9 December

the 'entire chain of command must remain under the political control and strategic direction of the EU throughout [any proposed] operation, after consultation between the two organisations', and that 'the operation commander will report on the conduct of the operation to EU bodies only'. As for NATO, it will merely be 'informed of developments'.

The EU is investing in the Galileo Satellite project, not because there is no effective satellite positioning system available, but because the only such system is under the control of the United States. Moreover, by allowing the Chinese to acquire a 15% share in Galileo, the EU has sent a striking message of repudiation to the Americans, who are averse to pooling military resources with China.

The current conduct of operations in Afghanistan exemplifies even better the Europe-NATO split. These operations were mandated by the UN and fully endorsed through NATO's internal procedures. Once begun, however, the engagement fragmented along national lines. The Germans refused to allow their forces to be moved into the more dangerous theatre of operation. The French Special Forces were withdrawn. And what remained was a 'coalition of the willing', of the kind that we should expect when cold determination at last prevails over hot air. Only the Dutch and the Danes aligned themselves with the British, the Australians, Canadians and Americans in the hard fighting.

The lessons from such episodes are clear. A national government can send its citizens to fight and die in defence of the nation. It can send them to fight alongside allies, since that too is a way of defending the nation and its vital ties. But it cannot send its citizens to fight and die for a cause that is not their

2000, Appendix to Annex VII to Annex VI, Annex to the Permanent Arrangements on EU/NATO Consultation and Co-Operation on the Implementation of Paragraph 10 of the Washington Communiqué (3)

own and which bears little or no relation to the historical ties on which their hopes and loyalties are founded. We should not be surprised, therefore, at the failure of the EU to assert itself in any of the military conflicts. Judged from deeds rather than words, the EU would seem to be unable to form a self-contained alliance among its Member States. On the other hand, NATO is the world's most successful alliance, the only alliance in modern times that has been able to face down and defeat a massively armed enemy without firing a shot. It has also sheltered and made possible the growth of democracy in Turkey, the only Muslim country that enjoys Western-style accountability; it has assisted in the arming of Germany while confirming Germany's status as a peaceable member of the community of nations.

It is impossible to say, until it is too late, that a given defence policy has failed. But it is surely true that, by contrast with the policies pursued over 50 years by NATO, the policy of the EU is heading for failure. In any of the dire scenarios that we can now envisage, it is unlikely that a European force under European command would do anything substantive to protect us. Whether it be peace-keeping in the Middle East, taking the fight against terrorism to the enemy bases in Afghanistan and Somalia, destroying weapons of mass destruction or the capacity to use them, it is clear that the skill, courage and commitment necessary to carry through these dangerous tasks can be fostered only at the national level, by recruiting young people to the defence of their country and inculcating the values and loyalties without which it is impossible willingly to die in the service of others.

The dither and doubt that we witnessed over Bosnia and Lebanon will not be overcome by a European reaction force, however 'rapid', since it stems not from a deficiency of means but from a deficiency of ends. The European institutions don't know what to do, where to go or what to aim at in a conflict, for the very reason that the many national interests point in many directions. Only a constantly negotiated alliance can solve the problem of joint action and common defence; and to achieve this, the one thing nation states cannot do is subordinate the imperative of survival to the political goal of union.

Lydia was unimpressed: 'Your argument', she said, 'really points in the opposite direction from the one you intend. I grant that NATO has provided us, for the last 50 years, with the defence shield that we needed. But NATO belongs to the past. It will continue to exist, like the WEU, but it will become over-burdened and frustrated by all the tasks imposed on it. When we need to work alongside the Americans, we will do so through NATO, but there will be many times where a NATO or American-led force would not be able to carry out a complex political mission, whereas Europeans could. As you yourself claim, alli-ances must be constantly re-shaped, so as to meet the changing threats to their members. Is it wise for the European nations to remain dependent for their defence on an alliance whose most important member is not merely situated on the other side of the Atlantic Ocean, but increasingly detached from the under-standings that made the alliance possible? The people of Europe are largely hostile to American foreign ventures, to America's very ideological brands of democracy and capitalism, and to its policy of changing regimes when it should be changing hearts and minds. In these circumstances, it is surely imperative for the people of Europe to form a new and more localized alli-ance; and the EU provides them with the political structures and logistical competence that would make this possible. The nation states may be the only political entities that can easily ask us to die for them; but they stand and fall together, as we know from the European wars. Surely, it is now urgent to give the European people the ability to defend themselves, with-out exposing them to all the anger and hostility that are rightly

directed against America? I believe that Europe should be the
mechanism whereby the aggregated power of the European
states is organized effectively in pursuit of the enhanced security and protection of the European citizen.'

It was my turn to express doubt. Lydia, I suggested, had got
things back to front, like the whole approach to defence issues
by those of her persuasion; for they really don't rate threats to
European security high enough to justify real investment. So
the military arm is a tool for fulfilment of other ambitions. In
military matters, it seems to me, aspiration must take second
place to reality. The rhetoric surrounding the idea of a European
defence policy is full of aspiration; but it contains precious little reality. What we see, in any conflict, is the continuing desire
of the Member States to maintain control of their defence and
foreign policy. Even if they refer to goals that they describe in
high-toned sentences as 'European', they are almost always the
goals prescribed by national interest. As Bismarck expressed
it: 'I have always found the word "Europe" on the lips of those
who wanted something from other powers, which they dared
not demand in their own name.' That, it seems to me, is an apt
summary of the debate about European defence.

But Lydia is a lady of conviction. She largely ignored my
reservations and shifted the focus of the argument: 'Your fixa-
tion on defence and military matters misses the changed nature
of security in the 21st century. We are witnessing the re-emer-
gence of a multi-polar world with a decline of America's power
where military might on its own is no longer a guarantee of
success. This world is marked by terrorism and the prolifera-
tion of weapons of mass destruction, the damaging of the environment and the growing divide between the 'haves' and the
'have nots'. In such a security climate, it is soft power that matters. And here Europe's ability to set international standards,
its weight as a trading partner, its generosity as provider of

development assistance and capacity to intervene in complex emergencies are its greatest strengths and, ultimately, its best defence. Soft power, expressed for example through the European Commission's agencies for international aid and humanitarian relief, such as The European Commission Humanitarian Aid Office (ECHO), will ultimately give us greater security in a world moderated by reasonable agreement and the rule of international law than can ever be obtained by the sword or by national diplomacy.

But, sadly, we are not yet at this point. Military capabilities have to complement soft power with hard power. Because we are fighting the battle of the inner European space, we have forgotten that outside Europe lies a classical world in which military might is still the currency of power. A European army is still a necessary arm of the Union. And beyond its utility, I welcome such an army for its role in reinforcing European identity. I believe that it will be used as a force for good. Its time has now come. It is logical that the Americans, who have preoccupations elsewhere, will retreat from Europe because of their changed strategic interests. The paradox for Europeans is that if we are to make Americans less military, we have to become more military ourselves. Europeans will have to take up the burden for their own defence and so it should be. This is a normal, necessary and indeed fundamental task of any polity and the emergent European entity is no exception. Through our industrial and defence policy, we have been able to make a useful start in collaborating with major players outside our continent. You criticize Galileo as folly: I see it as a hopeful pioneer in giving Europe independence from the US in the crucial area of space and satellite communications. It is a good example of what distinguishes Europe's progressive approach to security from America's. By involving China, we are building friendly ties that will help safeguard Europe from the dangers posed by the emergence of another, as yet unpredictable, world power.

And then there is the threat of terrorism and cross-border movements which affect our internal security. These risks we have to face together. Worryingly, the harmonization of internal security is less far advanced than that of the military. The resistance of isolated Member States is understandable but unhelpful. It is irritating that a country like the United Kingdom should oppose majority voting in "Justice and Home Affairs" despite producing most of the initiatives in this area! But we do have in EuroJust the institutional foundation for a future European FBI. It will harmonize investigation, the issuing of warrants and, ultimately, of common immigration and border policies. Could you imagine any institution apart from the Union able to coordinate internal security? The consequences of the Single Market or Schengen make their national management impossible. I am hopeful that the Europeans are well on the way to taking responsibility for their own defence and security.'

I always admire Lydia's enthusiasm but she can often appear naive. And in matters touching on intelligence services, internal security and the military, she is dangerously so. With good reason, most countries – not only the British, but also France and Denmark, to name but a few – have shown a marked reluctance to pool relevant resources through the institutions of the EU. Collaboration in the area of policing and intelligence-sharing among European states continues to be based on old-fashioned, bilateral agreements (or, in the case of the Prüm Agreement, a multilateral agreement outside the realm of the EU), which are markedly effective in fighting cross-border crime and terrorism. Advances in the direction of a federal police force or a common intelligence gathering body will always be resisted as an intrusion into the most sensitive national prerogatives.

European defence needs may have to be re-thought. The old NATO structures, especially in view of French and German reservations, are insufficient to protect us. However, it is dangerous to pretend to powers – especially to military powers – which you do not have. It is more prudent to aim at a European defence that is built upon an alliance between separate but cohesive nation states, which can command the respect and loyalty of their citizens. The 'Remarkable or Paradoxical Trinity' of Clausewitz is still valid today. For any military operation to be successful, the state, the army and its leadership and the people have to be committed, well balanced and unified. All three corners of the triangle must compute or else the structure fails. If and when Europe is a single state, supported by a dedicated population, it will have, no doubt, its own army – but a merged army will not help make such a state.

LETTER 12

Enlargement

Some time ago, when Lydia and I looked together at the map of the continent, we wondered how far the European Union could expand. We have natural boundaries to the West, North and South, but not to the East. For Europe, obviously, includes the Balkans, as well as the Ukraine and Belarus, but what about the Caucasus? And Russia, with its overwhelming Asian hinterland? We both thought then that there was no rush, that we had ample time to ponder the question. Clearly, we failed to anticipate the seemingly irresistible momentum generated by the end of the Cold War.

Recent enlargement of the EU, to incorporate the newly liberated satellites of the Soviet Union, was a sudden and remarkable act. It was accomplished after the bare minimum of consultation with those – the people of the existing Member States – most likely to be affected by it. The decision was, however, by no means arbitrary; on the contrary, its logic was that of the original post-war project. The countries of central and eastern Europe had been maintained in a state of suspended animation since the Second World War; and the European Union, if it was to fulfil its role as the alternative to European belligerence, had to include them within its boundaries. The move was for the most part very much welcomed by the people of central and eastern Europe, and it is easy to see why. For the EU incorporated them virtually overnight into a viable capitalist economy, provided them with established legal principles and concepts in all the areas – commercial, civil, financial and property law – which had been destroyed or mutilated by the communists. The EU also opened them to the much-needed inflow of capital investment, some of it in the form of European Union subsidies. Most important of all, it brought central and eastern European countries back home to Europe. Undeniably, the move helped to stabilize the post-communist economies, and to give credibility to the emerging democratic structures. From many points of view, therefore, it must be counted among the European Union's successes that were deemed impossible when the European Commission first drafted a policy paper on enlargement in 1992.

Although we both think that some of the countries joined prematurely, Lydia does not share my more profound misgivings. I question whether there might not have been an equally successful and less costly alternative. The Treaty of Rome's guarantee of the free movement of labour has immediately surfaced as the highest of many costs not only to the original Member States, but also to those newly incorporated. Skilled workers from central and eastern Europe have moved in their many thousands to the West, depriving their countries of origin of human capital needed to achieve a genuine free economy. Lawyers, doctors, engineers, university professors and researchers – all are in critically short supply. And the attempt to build a rule of law and economic accountability in those countries where both had been deliberately destroyed is an ongoing struggle. The mass of EU regulations is no substitute for genuine legal procedures, and the lack of legal knowledge or trusted courts has meant that many indigenous businesses proceed in the old way, pretending to obey the regulations, but operating a black economy. At the same time, the regulations themselves, inherited from developed economies, which have adapted to take account of them, are naturally greeted with astonishment by people for whom law is something to be avoided and whose every commercial venture has hitherto been a shot in the dark. Their impact is felt in different ways at the top and at the bottom of society. The big players – often *ex-apparatchiki* who have enjoyed the benefits of privatization and their clients in government – can find a way round the more tedious rules. And there is not the slightest likelihood that they will transcribe European Directives into a seriously enforceable code of law. Take the Financial Services Action Plan. As an example, in the UK, this framework has already been translated into 1000 pages of rules and regulations, including elaborate provisions for inspection and enforcement, the whole likely to cost billions of euros in time-consuming and time-wasting employment. The likelihood that such a system of rules and regulations would be inflicted on themselves by the ruling powers in, let's say, Bulgaria is zero: there is not the motive, the infrastructure or the ability to meet the cost. At this level, therefore, European legislation is likely to be reduced to a compact ball of insignificant gestures.

By contrast, at the level of the small farmer and the self-employed contractor, the impact of regulation will be enormous, since such people are compelled to earn rubber stamps if they are also to earn their daily bread. As an example, consider the effect of European Health and Safety Directives on the traditional sheep farming economy of Romania. Old ways of making the sheep's milk cheese, old ways of curing it and selling it, and old ways of managing the herds have all been ruled out overnight, with no proven health benefits. According to Brussels, Romanian farmers may no longer bring down their flocks from the hills by herding them. They must find means to carry them in a more 'hygienic' way through a country-side ill-served by roads suitable for commercial livestock carriers. In short, that which is good in the old way of life based on sheer necessity – the local food economy, the integrity of rural areas, the robust self-sufficiency of the peasant farmers – becomes instantly vulnerable. That which is bad – the corrupt deals, the gargantuan projects, the massive flow of funds to unaccountable state officials and state projects – remains largely unaffected.

Lydia dismissed my observations as trivial and anecdotal. 'We all know perfectly well that some eastern European countries have been allowed in whilst still being far from meeting even the most generous interpretation of the minimum requirements. The report of the EU inspectors made it abundantly clear that a few months before their admission to the Union, corruption in Romania was endemic and mafia gangs operated with impunity in Bulgaria. In terms of economic performance, administering justice and complying with human rights legislation, they were equally far from meeting the criteria set by the EU. And, of course, it was a little silly of the Commission to expect the countries to put right in months what they failed to do in centuries. But does that matter? It will take years, perhaps many decades, before the standard of living will have evened out across the continent; before the political culture of a fully democratic society will be a matter of course every-where; before the European writ will run with equal force in Slovakia and Germany. But we will only achieve all this if we embrace the less fortunate countries within an aspirational Union, allowing them to assimilate gradually the high standards set with the active and generous support of the established sis-ter states. After bringing down the "Iron Curtain", we now have to tear down the "Silk Curtain" between us. I have no doubt that eventually Europe will have one law, one political culture, one economy with all Member States benefiting and contributing in equal measure.'

This may or may not be so, but I am not convinced that admitting candidate states too early into an essentially bureaucratic club will help, rather than hinder, their development. With the best of intentions, the EU has insisted on conformity to the European Convention on Human Rights, as interpreted by the Strasbourg Court, as well as to its own additional provisions requiring democratic elections, acceptable punishments, civilian government, non-discrimination and so on. The effect in some of the new Member States will be traumatic. To put the matter simply, the purpose of Enlargement was to bring order to central and eastern Europe. In fact it has brought a measure of entropy to both East and West; depriving the first of its skilled workers and threatening its fragile social and cultural capital, while putting unmanageable pressure on infrastructure, housing, employment, welfare provisions and educational resources in the second. There is a simple reason for these effects: the EU treaties are unsuitable to the circumstances in which we find ourselves. Total freedom of movement risks destabilizing the continent and centralization imposes an insensitive regimentation on post-communist economies. This web of well-intentioned regulations undermines the values which would enable people to take full advantage of their newly acquired freedom.

Here, Lydia interjected once more: 'You draw a pretty bleak picture. Yes, in the short term, enlargement causes serious difficulties, like non-compliance with common standards or discrepancies in values and standards of living. But, at the same time, each wave of enlargement has accelerated the political and economic development of new Member States. Fear of paralysis and disintegration acts as an instinctive driving force for more European integration.'

Lydia may be right, but she is talking about integration on

paper, not in practice. It looks good in Brussels, less good in Bratislava. Of course, it is too late to reconsider the terms of an enlargement that has already occurred, but what about the future? Whenever we discuss Enlargement, Turkey takes centre stage. The subject is complex. It is enveloped in great difficulties, but Lydia and I are largely in agreement as to the issues involved. There are many good reasons to have Turkey within the European Union and as many weighty ones not to include her. Some Member States resist this expansion, others promote it, but all recognize that the decision will define the character of the Union, whichever way it goes.

On the one hand, the presence of a major Muslim country enhances the liberal and open character of the Union and sends a positive message to our Mid-Eastern and North African neighbours. Turkey has been a faithful ally to Europe, a pivotal member of NATO in its confrontation with the Soviet menace throughout the Cold War. With such a powerful presence at the heart of the Middle East, Europe could play a significant role maintaining some sort of stability in that region so vital to our energy supply. Contrary to popular misconception, in Turkey secular jurisdiction *does* take precedence. It is Atatürk's great achievement that he banished the *ulema* and deprived them of their law-making powers. The law of Turkey, based on the *Code Napoléon*, has been European law for nearly a century. Why not incorporate into Europe the only Islamic nation that has learned to privatize its religion, and live by European ways? Isn't Turkey exactly the model that we would wish all Muslim countries to follow, and an example to our own Muslim minorities in Europe? In any case, do we have the right to exclude any country that feels itself to be truly 'European'?

On the other hand, the participation of a Muslim country of such dimensions dilutes, perhaps fatally, the Judaeo-Christian and cultural base on which the EU was founded. Unknowingly, the vast majority of the French start their day with the ritual murder of the Turk, when eating a 'croissant', originally baked to celebrate the lifting of the siege of Vienna. Turkey is, for the most part, situated in Asia Minor, with a past not remotely connected to the inner history of our continent. It has a large, young and relatively impoverished workforce, ready to transfer itself as soon as it can to the cities of Europe. And would it not be an act of military folly to set the border of Europe in the world's more volatile region, with Syria and Iraq as close neighbours? Although the secular law takes precedence, it is the army that safeguards this law in times of chaos and is always ready to step in when Atatürk's constitutional provisions are threatened. But membership of the Union will deprive the army of its role, so Islamic parties could emerge and set about dismantling the secular state. It is even possible to envisage a scenario where Islamic parties, joined together across the whole European electorate, would become the largest coherent block in the European Parliament. Would that not mean an irreversible change to European identity?

My impression is that, on the whole, Lydia is in favour of Turkey's adoption, especially because promising Turkey the possibility of membership only to say 'no' now would have a devastating effect on the standing of Europe in the Muslim world. After all, the famous article in the 1963 Association of Union offering Turkey the possibility of membership was put in not at Turkey's but at European request. She seems to be attracted by the larger picture based on higher aspirations: in geopolitical terms, a cohesive Greater Europe, with a population of some 500 million (theoretically approaching 600 million with Turkish membership), with a relatively high GDP and its industrial, commercial, financial and military might, would be a genuine world power, sitting comfortably at the top table with the US, Russia and the rising empires of China and India. In a globalized world, the stakes are measured in the unforgiving currencies of energy, nuclear capability, raw materials, technical know-how and sheer mass. Her preference is, however, hedged by reservations and doubts not just about Turkey, but about the outcome of the enlargement process.

Whichever way you look at it, there is no satisfactory solution, either to the question of future enlargements or to solving the Turkish dilemma. The single framework, the all-or-nothing principle, the rigid treaties within which the EU has to live, simply do not allow it. Yet, to my mind, if the EU were to adopt a more flexible approach, the task of resolving an untenable situation would become less intractable. This is why we must avail ourselves, as soon as possible, of a new European structure, one based on the principle of real subsidiarity. The power to take this kind of decision must be recaptured by the nation states. It should not be a power exercised by a central body, nor should it have such radical geo-political effects. If the EU were a union of sovereign nation states, supported by multilateral agreements with the external world, there could be no reason why it should not be extended in any direction we please. Turkey could be a member, Syria, Lebanon, maybe the entire Middle East and North Africa. Extensive trading agreements have existed before now between Islamic and European powers. But they have not been pushed in the direction of an exchange of populations, an adoption of unified laws, or a pooling of sovereignty.

I cannot honestly see how these dichotomies can ever be reconciled unless we adopt a multi-dimensional structure with a basic minimum membership criterion and an opportunity to opt into various spheres of deeper integration.

LETTER 13

Demography and Immigration

The extent and pace of structural changes in the population profiles within European societies pose some of the most severe challenges of the 21st century. They jeopardize long-standing expectations, tacit agreements and legally guaranteed promises on which people have come to depend. Two fundamental changes in particular need to be addressed: the shift in the demographic balance and the effects of mass immigration.

Lydia believes instinctively that all difficulties experienced by Member States, when similar in character, could best be alleviated by common strategies implemented centrally through the European Union. She understands full well that the dramatic decline in the working population as a proportion of the total is placing a rapidly growing burden on provisions of pensions and healthcare throughout the continent. And, according to her, the magnitude of the challenge cannot be met effectively by countries on their own. The sacrifices needed, the demands imposed on individual citizens disappointed in their expectations, will be more readily accepted if embodied in mandatory regulations that apply to the whole of the Union. The added, long-term benefit would be the standardization of these provisions so that those retired could live the rest of their lives, in comfort, anywhere of their choice. Would not that be worth the struggle? Would its achievement not redound to the credit of the Union with a corresponding appreciation of the EU by the people so lacking at present?

But the demographic problem is by no means uniform over Europe. Whilst the decline in the birth rate and increasing longevity may be a general phenomenon, the obligation every nation has to its individuals is varied across the continent. In France and Germany, state pensions backed by pay-as-you-go schemes were promised when life expectancy was ten years less than now under a situation close to full employment. It can soon no longer be fully delivered. In Britain, where the less generous state pension has been supplemented by extensive private schemes, the funding gap is less severe, even though heavy taxes recently imposed on private pension funds have devalued pensions there too. In Italy and Greece, where arrangements are more ramshackle and promises more vague, there is a prevailing sense that the extended family will provide, and that somehow, despite a striking decline in the birth rate, people will look after their own.

Now there are, it seems to me, only three options to address this problem: increase the age of retirement, so shifting taxation from the young to the middle aged; reduce the amount to be paid out as pensions; load up the overall level of taxation; or any combination of these three options. None of these options is easy – they will need all the arts of persuasion upon which a government can draw. But it will certainly be rejected if imposed by some *other* government than the one that represents the people who are being invited to accept it. The German government, for example, is in a strong position to persuade the Germans to accept the only policy that can save them from economic decline. It can describe the benefits that people have received from post-war social policies. It can argue that improved health has made it possible for people to work far longer than their parents did, without suffering ill effects. And it can point to the injustice of imposing on their own young the cost of comforts that the Germans had no birthright to expect. Already, indeed, this argument is being voiced in the German press, and it is surely the way forward. But it is a way that is available only at the national level, and only by invoking the decency and good will that are the natural by-products of public sentiment. Italy is an altogether different case. Although Italians, to everyone's surprise, have suffered a near-terminal decline in their birth rate, the extended family remains in place as the principal network of social support. State provision has traditionally been distrusted, not only because of the constant devaluation of the currency, but also because of its erratic and uncertain nature. Hence, people have been in the habit of fending for themselves, and the instinctive kindliness of the Italian family has meant that few people are without the networks on which they can call in their time of need.

The prospect of a radical decline in the birth rate is not one that should be regarded with equanimity. Although raising the age of retirement does provide a partial remedy, there will come a moment of danger when many things that depend on young people – not least policing and defence – are seriously jeopardized. The French government faced this problem in the 1950s and '60s and introduced incentives, reinforced more recently, designed to encourage women to have children with the opportunity to continue to work. And, after a period of population decline, France has experienced a rise in birth rates sufficient to restore confidence in the possibility of a fiscal solution to the pension crisis. There is also some evidence that population declines are cyclical, so that below a certain point a society will spontaneously move back towards a condition of replacement.

Lydia is not slow to remind me that free migration within the Union goes some way towards ameliorating the demographic conundrum. For it is primarily the young generation that moves to augment the workforce in countries in dire need of skilled and unskilled labour. The British economy, for example, would not have been half so successful in the absence of a major central and eastern European contribution. As she put it, 'the ramifications of the Single Market are manifold. One of its key provisions is the free movement of citizens of all Member States within the Union to seek and accept employment, not subject to any national discrimination. This provision is not accidental. Its function is to rationalize the human resources of Europe so that unemployment and underemployment are brought into balance throughout the continent. So an over-abundance of Polish plumbers and Romanian doctors can fill yawning vacancies in the West where their technical abilities are more than welcome. Such movement of labour, affecting immigration within the Union, seems to be preferred by most to importing people from other continents whose cultural and social assimilation poses far greater challenges.'

This is true, at least in some measure, with respect to all the wealthier nations. But sudden migration on such a scale comes at a cost. For the incoming labour consists of people who, under the EU treaties, have rights to claim social, educational, housing and medical benefits on a par with the local population. The sheer scale of population movements in itself creates more problems than it solves. The British Home Office anticipated the arrival of 55,000 migrant workers from Poland on the latter's entering the European Union. In the event, the figure turned out to be ten times greater. Panic measures have been adopted by the governments of France, Germany, Britain and now Italy, in order to arrest the flow of economic migrants from central and eastern Europe. But the measures are probably illegal under the Treaties, and could soon be undone by the courts. The problem then arises of how to manage the enormous strain on infrastructure and on the collective savings of the host communities whose friendly feelings towards incomers claiming benefits, towards which they have, *a fortiori,* made no contribution, cannot be taken for granted.

If the result of EU intervention in people movement within the Union is doubtful, its legislation in the realm of illegal immigration from outside, by implication, is wholly detrimental. There are currently upwards of a million illegal immigrants in Spain, whose government is contemplating an amnesty, granting citizenship to all of them. Such a course of action is in the national interest, for with Spanish citizenship the immigrants will be able to settle anywhere in the Union, and the burden of providing for them will no longer fall only upon Spain. But this means that other countries will be obliged to treat these migrants as legal residents, whatever their provenance or their social contribution.

What has become clear to most objective observers of European affairs is that the Union is part of the problem, not part of its solution. Migration, internal or external, legal or illegal, is the concern of each nation state. Only the nation states have the means to integrate the newcomers into the indigenous community and the ability to ensure that the social, economic and cultural impact of these unprecedented migrations can be weathered by the people. And it is highly unlikely that the nation states will react in the same way. Poles and Italians, who share their religious heritage and their distrust of politics, have an ability to integrate that is not shown by the British and the Romanians, for example, or the Slovaks and the French. Each nation state will have its own preference among the migrant populations, and its own way of striving to absorb them. Dublin is now home to the second biggest urban population of Latvians after Riga. However, as they address themselves to this problem, the nation states of Europe will be ever more aware that the binding principles of the Treaty of Rome, which tie their hands at a critical moment in their national history, belong to another epoch and another crisis. The *ad hoc* measures currently adopted by the national governments will come up against the 'irreversible' demands of a Treaty signed by other men in other times, singularly unhelpful in the current circumstance.

Lydia, ever hopeful, dismissed my estimation of the situation as a snapshot of the inevitable difficulties that occur in every transitional phase. She saw the profound differences in the condition and needs among Member States as temporary imbalances. To her mind, with the help of the Union's redistribution of benefits, the poorer countries will soon catch up with their wealthier neighbours, offering sufficient employment opportunities to keep people at home. But on the subject of illegal influx from beyond the borders of Europe, Lydia is always passionate. 'There are enormous pressures of immigration from Africa and Asia of people who are desperate to escape from their war-ravaged, drought-plagued and impoverished countries to find a decent home in Europe. There is no prospect of this pressure abating. It is very likely that it will become more intense. If the defences of any country are breached, it affects all the Member States simply because immigrants established in the country of their entry are free to move on and settle anywhere on the continent. Spain alone cannot cope with boatloads of refugees landing in the Canary Islands, nor Britain with multitudes awaiting their chance in ports across the channel, nor Poland with economic migrants infiltrating its porous eastern borders. Whether these migrants are legal or illegal, asylum seekers or ambitious opportunists, the challenge is to Europe and it is Europe, as a whole, which has to meet it. In the 21st century the issue of immigration can no longer be neatly apportioned to individual nation states, it has to be a European deal.'

'Migration', she continued 'is the norm of settlement. People move around the planet, from the places that cannot support them to the places that can. The idea that migration is both a challenge and a security threat, which has developed in Europe in recent years, not only denies fundamental European values; it also goes counter to the history of the continent. Europe is the product of different waves of people who arrived to build an area of peace, of fundamental values and of ideals. It has always been a place where people came and went, which explains the strength of the European peoples. Their complex genetic inheritance has adapted them to our varied landscape and temperate climate. Others are now coming, and there is every reason to suppose that they too will adapt. Stefan Zweig's *Memories of a European* is a fantastic book that forms part of my vision. He explains that at the end of the 19th century and the beginning of 20th century until the First World War, people circulated freely in Europe. It was not the EU that created an area without borders. The greatest danger to the European project today is the rise of xenophobia, the refusal of the 'other', the banalization of discriminatory attitudes. Immigration becomes a problem precisely when it is seen in *national* terms – as a threat to *us* from *them*. And if you look at the French response to the suburban riots you will see that what success it had was due precisely to the fact that issues of race, nationality and ethnicity were not mentioned in the official account of things. The rioters were treated as fellow citizens, obliged to obey the law and entitled to its protection like any other French person. I am certain that immigration would be less of a problem if the burden were genuinely shared. It is precisely the national feelings and identities that get in the way. Each country tries to pass on the burden to its neighbour, as the Italians do with their policy of internment, designed to encourage Albanians to move on to France. A genuinely European policy would involve strict control of Europe's external borders, and total freedom of movement within them. This would unite the nations in the attempt to ease tensions while migrants move to more receptive locations and less overcrowded occupations best suited to their culture and their skills.'

Lydia's vision is compelling until we reflect upon the facts. There is nothing in the integrationist scheme of things to help the overseas newcomer to assimilate to any one national culture that surrounds him or her. The most striking feature of the European response to the growing tension between immigrant and host country is that the much-vaunted European identity is never mentioned. Mainstream politicians have been very shy of urging our immigrant communities to adapt to the European, rather the national, form of life. No reference is made to an obligation to understand and adopt the Enlightenment values whose good effects they have come to enjoy.

We know, from recent elections and emigration statistics, how the French, Dutch, German or Austrian people, to name a few, feel about the immigration policies that have been put in place by previous generations of politicians. But we also know that the EU will do nothing to help the peoples of Europe to solve the immigration difficulties that their countries now confront. Not only the search for the solution, but the solution itself depends upon national effort and national identity. Immigrants cease to be disaffected, and no longer define themselves as 'apart from' their hosts, only when they have been integrated into the surrounding society. And in our European case, the 'surrounding society' manifestly means the nation. The problems faced, for example, by the Dutch will be solved only when those of Moroccan and Indonesian ancestry define themselves as *Dutch*, identifying themselves through the language, culture

and landscape of The Netherlands. It is when they form friend-
ships, grant and receive favours, and organize their lives on the
assumption that the 'we' to which they belong is precisely the
same 'we' as their indigenous neighbours, that they will have
truly settled.

   This point, so obvious that it hardly needs making, nevertheless places a large question mark over the project of European
integration. If anything, it is increasing pressures, not reducing them. The resolution of the current crisis does not involve
marginalizing the nation state but, on the contrary, enhancing
its status, its visibility and its identity-forming role. It is all that
we have by way of a path to social integration. And to despise it,
to set it aside as some kind of atavistic survival, is to guarantee
the non-belonging and permanent alienation of our immigrant
communities.

LETTER 14

Protecting the Environment

Lately, the struggle to control climate change has moved to the centre of the global agenda for the 21st century. For Lydia, such a topic was precisely where her vision of Europe was superior to mine. She spoke with passion: 'While I concede that social issues may be issues with frontiers that can be addressed on a national basis, environmental problems, by contrast, are without borders. They concern changes in our world that have multinational effects. There can be no meaningful response to the damage caused by carbon emissions, which is not also a concerted, trans-national, action. The environment is a cause looking for a champion and the EU is a champion looking for a cause. So it is, therefore, right that they have found each other. It is right too that the EU comes to be seen, in particular by the next generation, as the Environment Union. It is in the lead protecting the world from this new great threat.

The unfolding struggle for climate control is without parallel in the long human story. We do not have much time in which to marshal our forces. Therefore, the EU, with the authority to legislate for a whole continent, has both the

motive of self-interest and also a wider global responsibility
to protect the environment. I am proud of the Commission
for taking this task so enthusiastically to heart and promoting the Union as the leading test-bed in the world. In creating
new forms of trans-national accords and setting legally binding
targets to curb the emission of greenhouse gases, the EU has
taken the leading role in world affairs. The EU took the moral
high ground at the Bali Climate Conference although sadly it
was defeated by the wilful selfishness of the USA.'

'Yours is a stirring evangelical account, Lydia,' I replied,
'but the inconvenient truth is that it simply is not so. Take what
you say about the Bali conference. Yes, the EU was defeated
and thank goodness that it was, for the sake of the environment. The EU was promoting an even more stringent version
of a bankrupt approach, the so-called Kyoto mechanism. That
mechanism of top-down, output-target, mandatory treaty had
failed to make any difference in practice in ten years. But, as
in other areas of such top-down *dirigisme*, the EU response has
been to demand more of what has just failed.

However, the failure of the EU approach to climate policy is
instructive in more detail, not least because the facts are so little known. As you rightly say, the EU desired to promote itself
as the world leader on climate policy. Therefore, it rushed to
introduce the world's most ambitious carbon trading scheme,
the EU Emission Trading Scheme (ETS). Under its terms, firms
were given (or in the later version, could buy at auction) trade-
able permits for the right to emit carbon. Under the first version of the EU ETS, governments allocated these permits to
their industries. Unsurprisingly, many saw this as a windfall
subsidy. So the Italian Government, for example, dished out to
Italian industry permits to the equivalent value of all Europe's
estimated carbon emission. In May 2006, the price of such permits duly crashed from 30 euro/ton to a few cents. There is no

successful example of creating a genuine commodity market by Directives from above.

Where reductions have happened, notably in eastern Europe, in re-unified Germany and in the UK, they were the result of policies unrelated to climate change. In the former cases, collapsing communism and with it, highly inefficient and polluting industries, reduced emissions. In the latter, Mrs Thatcher's smashing of union power, by destroying the British coal industry, substituted coal with North Sea gas in the 'dash for gas'. Strip out Germany and the UK from the EU-15, and between 1990 and 2005 European emissions actually increased 10%. Governments wishing to appear 'green' thus need to obtain extra-European offset credits via the Kyoto 'Clean Development Mechanism' (CDM) through which big emitters can claim credits for reductions bought in developing countries. Vast scams, accounting for two-thirds of all contracts agreed under the CDM until 2012, have enabled profiteers to make big money without materially reducing emissions or helping the world's poor. These include prime examples such as making potent green-house gases (by-products of manufacturing refrigerants), then destroying them and selling the credits for doing so at great profit.

All in all, the inconvenient truth is that the EU carbon trading has imposed no control on emissions and has no real prospect of doing so. Instead, it has become a money machine for sharp dealers and has created a devoted market of such people and a forum for 'green' activists who try to impose more onerous regulations and taxes on European industry *via* the European Parliament, moves fiercely resisted by national governments. When the rubber hits the road, governments have refused to cripple the airline sector as the climate puritans would wish. And Chancellor Merkel made it indignantly plain that Germany would resist EU regulations that would destroy its high-end motor manufacturing industry.

Consider a different damaging by-product of modern prosperity: packaging. This case reveals the flaws in your vision of
Europe in other ways. Non-biodegradable packaging is now
entering the environment at such a rate that landfill sites will
soon no longer be able to contain it. All over Europe, fields,
rivers, lakes and hedgerows are filling with plastic bottles and
bags; and 25% of the weight of every shopping bag that leaves
the supermarket consists of yet more of the stuff. Yet what is the
reaction of the EU? To require all food to be packaged before it
can leave the farm; to lay down stringent health and safety regulations that cannot be met by small local shops. Food must be
packaged in plastic. It obliges manufacturers to wrap detailed
instructions in ten languages along with all their products. In
general, it forces upon producers and consumers across the
Union a culture of litter and waste. No national government
that wished, now, to get rid of non-degradable packaging and
to return to the benign regime of sweets in paper bags, fish in
newspaper, or pickled beets in barrels, could do so. Everybody
throughout the Union has been locked into practices of production and distribution of food, which have a long-term environmental cost. This will far outweigh the short-term benefits for
the health of consumers. The entirely contradictory responses
of the EU to carbon emission and packaging waste is unfortu-
nately symptomatic of the fault lines of all highly centralized,
over-bureaucratic governments. When faced with difficulties
they issue instant edicts, create a raft of regulations, deal with
each difficulty on its own, disregard any fall-outs, admit no mistakes and never reverse a course once taken.'

Lydia's brow furrowed. But the facts and figures are what
they are. So she moved to different ground to reinforce her
case. 'Do you not value the quiet revolution all around the
coastline of Europe? Did our clean beaches come by accident?
No, they are clean thanks to European regulations. It was the

Water Directive from Brussels that forced local authorities to clean up their act. European beaches have improved beyond recognition. People are safer and more confident both at sea and on dry land with a corresponding benefit to the leisure and tourist industry: a wholly positive outcome.'

I readily agreed on the outcome. That the beaches improved as a result of Brussels' intervention is not in doubt. But I asked myself whether the intervention was most effective because of the element of compulsion, backed by fines or threats of fines, or whether it would have been just as effective and much more efficient for Brussels to have used a far lighter touch to have set standards and monitored performance. Surely, if the public was adequately informed of how hygienic and unsullied a beach was in relation to other beaches, it would make a rational choice, and holiday resorts would have to react to save their very existence? The point, I suggested to Lydia, might seem trivial in her chosen example, but, as with the weightier subject of climate policy, it carried a deep and serious philosophical point about the uses of power.

Environmental issues are to some extent the inevitable by-product of prosperity; but they are also the result of a fanatical concern for current well-being, which causes one generation to export the cost of its comforts to the next, in the form of pollution and waste. That is the lesson of the packaging and climate change stories. So I invoked an old dispute between two great Europeans, one an Irishman, the other a Swiss-born Frenchman, both European patriots, and both living and working away from their parental homes.

Edmund Burke's response to Jean-Jacques Rousseau's theory of the Social Contract was to acknowledge that political order is like a contract, but to add that it is not a contract between the living only, but between the living, the unborn and the dead. In other words, it is a relation of trusteeship, in which inherited benefits are conserved and passed on. The living may have an interest in consuming the earth's resources, but it was not for this that the dead laboured. And the unborn depend upon our restraint. Long-term social equilibrium, therefore, must include ecological equilibrium.

This thesis, which environmentalists are apt to express in terms of 'sustainability', is better expressed in Burke's way. For Burke reminds us of a motive that arises naturally in human beings, and which can be exploited for the wider purpose of environmental and institutional conservation. That motive is love and it leads people both to create good things and to destroy them. But it turns *of its own accord* in a direction that favours conservation, since human love extends to the dead and the unborn: we mourn the one and plan for the other out of a natural superfluity of good will.

The greatest weakness in environmental movements has been their failure to explore the question of human motivation, but rather to presume to know it; and it is a failure that is replicated in the European machine. There is one overwhelming reason for the degradation of the environment, and that is human appetite. In the wealthier parts of the world people are too many, too mobile, too eager to gratify their every desire, too unconcerned about the waste that builds up in their wake, too ready, in the jargon of economics, to externalize their costs. Most of our environmental problems are special cases of this general problem. And the problem can be more simply described as the triumph of desire over restraint. It can be solved only when restraint prevails over desire, in other words only when people have re-learned the habit of sacrifice. For what do people make sacrifices? For the things that they love. And when do these sacrifices benefit the unborn? When they are made for the dead. Such was the core sentiment to which Burke made appeal.

But how do we build that sentiment into a believable political programme? Surely not by a regime of Directives issued by a body that represents nothing dear to the subject to whom they are directed? The task of the politician is to gather the many feeble spurts of true benevolence, and to combine them in a continuous force, moving in a single direction. And there is a way of doing this, which is well familiar to us from a third great Enlightenment thinker.

So there was a Frenchman and an Irishman; but this point was best expressed by a Scotsman. He understood the fallibility in us all, and the importance therefore of attaching to moral incentives of love of others the internal motivator of self-love. Adam Smith's advice in *The Wealth of Nations* was that 'we address ourselves not to their humanity but to their self-love and never talk to them of our own necessities but of their advantages'. Link this most powerful and well-proven of political motivators to Burke's case – the advantages to which we will appeal then lie in Burke's transcendent case – and we have a hope of engaging self-starting political will: the only lasting kind.

Lydia was familiar with the drift of my thoughts. Yet her own conclusion moved in a different direction. 'Who can deny the proven record of Adam Smith's appeal to self-love? But this is both unimaginative and ignoble, Publia. It is no longer enough. It is always possible to appear profound when discussing the future of our planet, to invoke, as you do, the dead and the unborn. But now we will have to learn to love the whole of humanity directly and to embrace the whole of the world. The dangers to the environment are global. The response to them has to be on a global scale also. I accept that climate policy may not have worked well yet, but it is a good first step on a long journey. And your route is one I decline for logical as well as moral reasons.

International cooperation with multilateral agency is now the key. I remember when, in our youth, the Mediterranean was so polluted that you could not find a *rascasse* for your *bouill-abaisse*, still less an edible oyster or a healthy tuna fish. And the nations got together, under UN auspices, and cleaned up the place. They did it by adopting a policy of restoration instead of a policy of pillaging. That is how the tragedy of the commons, as the environmentalists call it, is overcome: by replacing competition by cooperation, and greed by care. It is what the EU could do, in a way that no temporary alliance of nation states could do in its stead. We both know how vital it is to ensure that principles of sustainability are introduced into economic globalization. I am surprised that you cannot see that the EU is without doubt the world's most promising organ to help accomplish that objective. The introduction of environmental norms lends itself more to the European model of business and industry than to the Anglo-American one, since it relies less upon the vagaries of an inherently volatile market. The EU approach to create large regulatory frameworks is the reality of existing Single Market linkages. If you do not set common standards, national regulations in the field of the environment can have competition-distorting effects. Now that the European vision is crystallizing into an "ever closer union", our gains are of benefit not only to ourselves but to the wider world.'

'I fully concur that principles of sustainability are to be welcomed,' I replied. 'Our disagreement is not of ends but of means. The real question is whether this cooperation can indeed be best achieved through the EU, with its built-in conflicts of national interest, or in some other way. When the Treaty of Rome was signed in 1957, the environment was not on the political agenda. Unsurprisingly, therefore, the regulatory regime derived from that Treaty makes it difficult if not impossible to address environmental problems. Consider then a further environmental example – the EU's performance over fisheries.

It is a matter of uncontested historical record that the Common Fisheries Policy was hastily put together when Britain and Denmark were applying for membership. Its driving purpose was not to protect European waters or the fish swimming in them. The indecent haste of its drafting was prompted by the opportunity to gain access for continental countries to the extensive and fertile marine resources of Britain and Denmark that put them in a different piscatorial category from other Member States. And the outcome has not been to conserve the stocks of British and Danish fish, but to exploit them. Thus 80% of EU fisheries are overfished; between 20-60% of catches are discarded in EU fisheries because of the 'Total Allowable Catch Regime'. Up to 90% of Scotland's catches have been discarded and 50% by volume and 70% by value of catches by the Dutch beam trawler fleet, compared to 4% discarded by Iceland and Norway, which have sovereign control over their fish stocks. The Fisheries Commissioner rightly stated that 'it is morally wrong to literally dump fish back into the sea. We are wasting a precious resource.' A leaked internal Commission report, stated that 'overcapacity, failure to stand up to special interests and a "command and control" system in Brussels have left fish stocks in many areas on the brink of collapse'. Nor does it even make money. The EU fishing fleets languish while those of New Zealand flourish.

Now fish stocks in European waters have fallen below the level of replacement. The only coastal waters in Europe where fish stocks are not in jeopardy are those of Iceland and Norway, countries able to protect their fish. Can you think of a more fully documented ecological disaster with a clearer culprit? This demonstrates that a founding principle of the European Community is potentially detrimental to the environment. The primacy of competition makes it possible for the EU to force countries in the name of the Single Market to adopt environmental protection standards which they would not have chosen themselves and which are counterproductive.

'You may dislike greatly those facts, as your face shows. But time will tell, as it always does,' I ended. 'Your prescription, dear Lydia, means another decade of hot air and inaction on climate policy and tons more unwanted plastic food packaging. It also signs the death warrant of European fisheries. Your belief that the EU is capable of directing sustainable environmental policy is a triumph of hope over experience.'

The Concluding Letter

Lydia and I were sitting once more in the *Campo dei Fiori*. It was now winter. A cold wind was blowing from the East across sombre skies. Lydia was late, her flight from Lisbon having been delayed due to some strike or other. The renamed Constitutional Treaty had been duly signed with pomp and ceremony by the Heads of all 27 Member States. Lydia's mood was strangely torn. On the one hand, while she was delighted at the progress of integration, she was frustrated that the document was neither as clear nor as incisive as she would wish; on the other, she was most uneasy about the way the deed had been done. Although not keen on referenda, Lydia's democratic instinct also told her that once people are consulted, to rebuff their verdict is inherently wrong. For myself, I was not surprised at the manner in which the constitution was imposed on the people of Europe. From the beginning, the guiding principle has been that the fewer contributors there are to decision making, the easier it is to realize the objective.

We ordered glasses of grappa. The wind was rising and rain squalls danced across the cobbles. I agreed with Lydia that this signing of the Lisbon Treaty was the right occasion on which to conclude the writing of these letters. I asked her how she would sum up her view of our conversations and this is what she said:

'From time immemorial, Europe has been the home of warring tribes, and later of warring peoples. Today it is a haven of peace. Ancient local antagonisms, as in Cyprus, Northern Ireland and the Basque country, remain, but even they are slowly being softened by the benign influence of Europe. The same effect is at work in soothing the intensity of the Left-Right divide in Europe's former communist and fascist dictatorships.

I agree that NATO and its nuclear shield have contributed to this peace. But it is increasingly recognized that today 'soft power' is the rising, leading form of power. Europe's soft power is of great international value, in its diplomatic experience, democratic credentials and moral authority. It has unrivalled historic connections beyond the continent: those of Spain with North Africa and Latin America; Britain with the Commonwealth; Austria and Germany with Central Europe; France and The Netherlands with their former colonies. No foreign countries know the Middle East as well as France and Britain. Does anyone want a world ruled unilaterally by the USA, or by a mutually suspicious USA and China, with the help of an unpredictable Russia and India? How would a Denmark, a Portugal, a Slovenia count in the world if not through the EU? Only a unified Europe, acting cohesively as a force for diplomatic solutions could bring some sanity and stability to the world.

Many cynics dismiss European unification as something founded on flags and anthems, or petty bureaucratic measures, like harmonized light bulbs. But the foundations are deeper than that. Democracy was invented in Greece, law in Rome. Both were reborn in Britain. Civilization without France and Italy would be immeasurably impoverished, music without Germany a minor art. Can you imagine painting without Velazquez and Rembrandt, or literature without Shakespeare? At the popular level, there is scarcely any youngster who does not follow European football avidly, with its heroes playing for Real Madrid, AC Milan or Manchester United. Meanwhile, the USA's orientation is shifting inexorably towards the emerging Pacific powers. As we become less important to America, so America will become less important to us as contributors to what used to be called 'leadership of the Western world'.

The so-called 'democratic deficit' is no worse in the EU than in most Member States. Composition of parliamentary lists; deals brokered behind close doors between party chiefs to assemble fleeting coalitions; prime ministerial tenures that increasingly resemble presidential ones, suborning the civil service, the judiciary and the media are all corrosive of democracy and all are taking place in the domain of nation states. The top-down political management that critics find so objectionable in the EU is in the mainstream of European tradition. We have always been ruled by a political and academic class, which knew better what the people wanted. The idea of being ruled by consent, rather than governed, is something of an Anglo-Saxon eccentricity. Their bottom-up political style is confined to the Northern margins of the continent. In any case, when the European Parliament takes over most of the legislative functions of its national counterparts, to the world the EU will be a model of modern democracy, just as Westminster was in the 19th century.

For some, Brussels has become a byword for bureaucracy gone mad. It is associated with an endless stream of rules and regulations, mostly to no purpose. Nothing could be further from the truth. It is EU regulations that make the Single Market work, that enable labour, goods and capital to move freely all across the continent, that curtail monopolies, protect the health and well-being of the population and set limits to human exploitation. It is the same regulations that support neglected and impoverished regions and pave the way to a continent with the same high standard of living throughout. This advanced form of governance reconciles economic competitiveness with social fairness. That reconciliation permits the EU to pursue a policy of global free trade from a position of unrivalled internal strength and cohesion.

That there is a covert direction of travel is a constant accusation of conspiracy thrown at those of us promoting the European ideal. The direction is determined each day by the needs of the day as perceived by national interests. Fortunately, the treaty text allows such flexibility. If you look at the preamble of the 1957 European Community Treaty, with its oft quoted phrase of an 'ever closer union' between European peoples – not between countries, but between peoples, please note – you have the objective. It is very broad, it is very vague, it could be everything or it could be very little.

The shortcomings, the problems, the weaknesses, the failings of course I admit. They are all part of the formative pains of any ambitious enterprise. The whole history of Union can be viewed as a succession of crises. But fortunately, to date, the outcome has always been 'more Europe'. Those engaged in driving the project have proved very skilled in crisis management and there is every reason to believe that the EU will survive and overcome those ahead, so that does not concern me. What concerns me most, at present, is how little affection there is among the people towards the Union. The 2005 referenda rejection votes of the French and Dutch merely underline the negative feelings prevalent almost everywhere on the continent. This is in striking contrast to the high level of popular support that the European project enjoyed right up to the signing of the Maastricht Treaty in 1992, and it is due to a regulatory regime that people perceive to be oppressive and to a general unawareness of the benefits conferred by the EU. So what is the remedy?

The people will get used to the rules, as they always do. But we need to do a lot more to raise awareness about what the EU does for them and what Europe ought to mean. So, in schools and universities, significant parts of the curriculum should be devoted to specifically European matters. Every city should have an EU information centre, like a tourist office, to help people use and enjoy the opportunities Brussels brings. If this implies increasing the EU budget, so be it. The future promise of a unified continent is worth the price.'

Along with the intelligence of her character, what I admire most in Lydia is the steadfastness of her faith. Whatever the realities, whatever the inconvenient facts, they are dismissed as inconsequential or temporary flaws. She is a true believer and her religion is a uniformly unified Europe. It was Kant who suggested that it is the enlightened attitude which resolves conflicts by rational dialogue, and which invites the warring nations of the world to leave their quarrels and join in a common League. This is an interpretation of European Enlightenment fondly entertained by Lydia. But, also according to Kant, there is for her an inconvenient truth. Such an attitude is of no effect, he wrote, without 'republican government', by which he meant the territorial jurisdiction exerted by sovereign nation states accountable to, and representative of, their citizens. To say that Europe became a force in the modern world on account of the EU and its 'unifying influence' is to beg the question. Europe became a force in the modern world because the nation states of Europe finally overcame the belligerent nationalism that was launched by the French Revolution, exported by Napoleon, turned back on itself in Bismarck's revenge, and then repeatedly reaffirmed until its final defeat in 1945. Why give the EU credit for a military and moral victory that preceded its own existence?

No-one denies that the 'unifying influence' of the EU has been helpful in establishing the new world order, and in giving voice to the Enlightenment idea. But it has not been alone. There are other unifying movements that contributed to peace. The unity of the Scandinavian nations, which have not always been at peace together, is now indissoluble. It is a unity brought about by a shared cultural and linguistic inheritance that is interwoven in a way to which the EU can only aspire. The Atlantic Alliance saved Europe from the hegemony of the Reich and the Soviet Empire by manifesting a unity of ideology and action rare in the annals of history. The hostility of the EU to other forces of unification, like these, plainly has to do with attempts at self-legitimization through claims that it, and it alone, has been and is the broker of unity in Europe.

As for soft power, how I wish that it could soften the hearts and minds of fanatics and ruthless dictators! Soft power works only when backed up by the hard power that can enforce it. Hard power has come to us from the Atlantic Alliance, not from the EU. There are no good reasons to think that this will change. Without credible military force, whether in alliance with others or sanctioned by a legitimate international body, soft power is the 'pretend power' of the child who sticks out his tongue while clinging to his father's coat-tails. A posture of non-belligerence makes sense for Europe only because of the shelter provided by the Atlantic Alliance. So the soft power of Europe should be complementary to (and emollient of) American tendencies of over-reliance on force (I agree with Lydia in that characterization) within the shared community of the West: not an alternative to it. I fully agree that the connections between the European nations and their former colonies are diplomatic assets that should be used for all they are worth. The historical experience of France and Britain in dealing with the Ottoman Empire and conflicts in the Middle East gives those two nations a *locus standi* that the Americans will always lack. But it is the nation states of Europe, not the EU, that are the guardians and possessors of these European cultural, historical and diplomatic assets. And it is the European nation states alone that can use them to good effect.

Lydia raises the spectre of a new balance of power, between China and the USA, with Europe excluded since America's strategic interests are moving towards the Pacific basin. I doubt this. European civilization has found its most energetic outpost in America. China's attempt to introduce capitalism without democracy, and a trading economy with scant rule of law, can lead only to a temporary coincidence of interests between China and America. The heart and soul of America are turned in quite another direction. Visit an American city and what do you find? Concert halls dedicated to our classical music; art galleries full of paintings brought from our shores; universities filled by European scholars; and a legal system and religious consensus that owe everything to Europe.

Lydia is worried about the people's indifference towards Brussels. She attributes this negative attitude to lack of awareness, to an absence of Euro-centric education. I think the reason is more serious than that. People are naturally frustrated with an endless stream of regulations; but it is the *way* that these regulations are created that really offends them. This is the consequence of the EU's 'top-down' interpretation of subsidiarity that has been a recurring theme in these letters. One example, currently on the agenda, is designed to place temporary employees on the same footing with permanent ones. On its face it is a generous idea. But Germany, Britain and one or two other countries object to it since, in their view, it would lead to serious job losses, yet they are powerless to block the initiative. EU decisions taken by qualified majority voting leave national parliaments impotent and their citizens disenfranchized. Worse than that, the EU consideration of this measure is based not on its own merit, but as part of a package on unrelated employment matters, so the result is dependent on behind-the-scene horse trading between the leaders of the Member States.

The task of translating the decisions taken by a congress of political leaders into rules is assumed by a powerful administrative centre with its own political ambition. Yet the implementation of the rules is transmitted to the nation states, together with the expense of complying with them. The electorates of Germany and Britain will never understand why they can have no say in the matter. This is exactly how the disastrous fishing policy of the Union came into being, more concerned as it was not with the preservation and cultivation of maritime Europe but with enforcing this policy as the British entry fee into the EC. So the issue is not about the rights of temporary employees or about the sustainable management of European fisheries. The common denominator is that decisions are not taken on the merits of the case. This is the true meaning of the 'democratic deficit' and it forms part of the very essence of the Union's current way of life.

The 'democratic deficit', with the consequent alienation of the people is, of course, not accidental. It is the built-in feature of a structure designed for one purpose: the standardization of a continent, the homogenizing of its economy and the integration of its political instruments. Here we come to the heart of the matter. Whatever topic Lydia and I touched on, the difficulties of the EU stemmed from one source. Riding alongside the incompatible interpretations of subsidiarity, the immense diversity of the Member States has been the other recurring theme of our inquiry. Be it economic life, politics, defence, population size, immigration, foreign affairs, standard of living, law and administration of justice, the gaps are simply too vast. To ask Denmark to merge its military forces is not the same as to ask France; to demand compliance with financial regulations from Hungary is not the same as demanding it from the City of London; to expect Common law countries to work with the European Court of Justice is not the same as expecting that from countries whose judicial traditions are based on Roman law; to impose fishing constraints on Austria is quite different from imposing them on Portugal; the protection of ethnic minorities has a different meaning in Germany and Romania. This is what stalls the process of integration and limits its extent. Trying to fit an asymmetric continent into a rigid, symmetric, one-dimensional frame is the single, most critical, cause of the Union's failures. The headlines of European unification sound grand. The price is in the small print. And the major players are increasingly reluctant to pay it. The independence of decision-making and freedom of action for a successful nation state are too precious to sacrifice. The parliaments of states with a reasonably good democratic record will not willingly relinquish any more of their powers in the foreseeable future.

That integration by standardization is grinding the unification of Europe to a standstill is not an original observation. Think-tanks in France, Britain, Germany, Holland and Belgium have all declared their deep dissatisfaction with the European institutions. In 2006, the *Conseil d'Analyse Economique* even described the current situation as 'perilous', an extraordinary judgement, coming from an authoritative French state institution. Roman Herzog, the former President of Germany, has condemned the centralizing and unaccountable machinery of the EU, and repudiated the Constitutional Treaty as advancing the contradictory and opaque structures which are responsible for the Union's current problems. President Klaus of the Czech Republic is well known to be hostile to the integrationist agenda and important voices in his country are now demanding radical change. The elite there is deeply split.

According to Lydia, few of her friends still overtly support the idea of a fully integrated federation. But this is to mistake the essence of my concern. Whatever they may think or say they think, the institutions and signed documents point in one direction only. The momentum can either stop or can continue to its preordained destination. There is nowhere else to go.

The process that led to the signing of the Lisbon Treaty – the Constitution in a cloak – is a clear signal that the European leaders do not care what people think. The decision to defy public opinion was, in my view, an even greater strategic error by the integrationists than holding referenda that are lost; for history indicates that the people of Europe will turn against an unpopular Union, bereft of legitimacy, in greater numbers and more intensely, as time goes on.

Concentration of central authority in few hands, a 'hold from above', has a poor record in modern history. The crisis to which the institutions of Europe were a first response was the result of one thing above all – the dictatorial approach to politics. Yet it is this same hold from above that has been built into the European process, which has one and only one way forward, namely 'more laws, more rules, more government, more power to the centre'. The dangers attendant on this concentration of powers are not aggressive, military or totalitarian. They are subtle and insidious. These are the dangers of civic alienation, of economic decline, and of the domination of decision-making by an increasingly unaccountable few.

Even the transient success of various dictatorships was conditional on having real power: an army, a police, a subservient legal arm, a tight grip on the economy, on the media and consumer supply. Despite having the power to fine, and the nuclear option to expel a Member State from the Union, the EU has none of these. It depends entirely on the goodwill of the nation states, the consent of their parliaments and, ultimately, on their electorates. Without popular support it has no future. Seen in the long view of history, the Lisbon ceremony may well have set back European unification for generations.

I sincerely hope that that European Union does not disintegrate, although it could. It would be sad if the prodigious effort sunk into creating a first organ for permanent inter-continental cooperation were to go to waste. But to save the Union we will all have to recognize that the simple, one-dimensional model cannot work. Many alternative models have been considered over the years. But the quasi-religious fervour for absolute integration has blocked objective evaluations of them. Now is the time to look for a viable plan B. As a starting point, we could do worse than be guided by what is actually happening.

The eurozone is an important feature of the Union without all Member States being compelled to join it. It may suit some countries better than others; it may or may not ultimately succeed; but in any case its demise would not necessarily mean the end of the EU. Or another example. France, Germany, Britain and now Italy have taken steps to limit movement of labour from central and eastern European countries. They have thereby contravened EU rules in their national interest. These 'transitional' measures are supposed to be temporary; but then so was the introduction of income tax by Pitt the Younger during the Napoleonic wars. One can go on. The Schengen Agreement, abolishing borders, overlaps only partially the territory of the EU. Initiatives towards joint military forces may or may not be the harbinger of a fully integrated European army, but the evolution of such an entity would not require a compulsory participation by Member States. In sum, the future points to an 'opt-in', rather than an 'opt-out', EU. In the future, there could, for example, be sub-unions in military cooperation, foreign affairs, the environment, regional regeneration, social policy and so on. Instead of grudging opt-outs, it would encourage a willing participation.

An 'opt-in' structure does not imply a simple *à la carte* model. That is the product of an opt-out Europe. Nor is it a 'two-speed Europe' where the distinction is merely one of timing in moving to full integration. Nor is it some sort of 'associate membership' of first and second-class citizens. An 'opt-in' structure means co-existing, partially overlapping alternative menus, that have sufficient flexibility to accommodate a fundamentally diverse continent without depriving its nations of their individuality.

The first priority to achieve an 'opt-in' Europe is to establish core areas of EU activity and to redefine the Copenhagen criteria for EU membership accordingly. The entrance requirement should be kept to a minimum, so as to permit 'developing' countries, like the Balkans, to join without carrying the full burden of the massive *acquis*, with which they cannot possibly comply in the foreseeable future. The low barrier, set at a suitably modified pre-Maastricht level, would also enable Turkey to become a full member, without threatening to unbalance the predominantly Christian culture of the continent. Belonging to a primarily economic union, members would have primarily economic benefits derived from free access to a market with a relatively affluent population of around 500,000,000.*

Such a structure does not have that aesthetic unity of a fully integrated Europe which is so ardently desired by Lydia. It is messy, fraught with difficulties and requires the courage of a radical re-think. The defining line between the mandatory Union and the voluntary 'opt-in' sub-unions would, no doubt, be the subject of massive disagreements. The relinquishing of some portions of the sacred *acquis* under true subsidiarity would no doubt be fiercely resisted. The transition of the EU

---

* The combined population of all 27 member countries has been estimated at 495,128,529 in January 2007.

institutions from a political to primarily an administrative centre is the work of years without any glamour and compensat-
ing glory. The scope of the ECJ would be limited strictly to the
functioning of the basic, minimalist Union and no court likes
to have its area of competence reduced. The budget of Brussels would inevitably contract to the detriment of the career
prospects of its functionaries and the net beneficiary countries.
The European Parliament would no longer be the ultimate
destination of a pan-European democracy with supremacy
over national parliaments. It might remain a useful forum for
political debate on matters of genuine continental concern. All
this is predicated upon a reversal of priorities from institution-
building, in anticipation of reality, to dealing with the realities
and allowing responses (which may sometimes include the creation of institutions) to arise thereafter.

I believe that such a flexible framework would serve the
future needs of Europe a great deal better than what we have at
present. But, with the upheaval involved, I am not naive enough
to recommend it on its merits alone. I put it forward because it
is simply the only alternative to a failed integrationist agenda.
The higher the project of integration aims in theory, the more
certain is a break-up in practice. Europe does not have the lux-
ury of presiding over its own slow disintegration, as the Union
runs into the sand.

What then should we do to preserve the civilization of
Europe? We must identify those features of our inheritance that
can still be offered to the young, and which will still attract
their loyalty. We must return to the people of Europe the great
gifts that their ancestors brought to mankind: self-government,
citizenship and freedom under law.

We parted: Lydia north to her apartment near Piazza
Navona and I to walk back to my hotel on the Aventine. Night
had fallen and the earlier squalls had given way to a fine drizzle.

Tired waiters framed in the glaring restaurant windows were
stripping tables and clearing away chairs. A cat slunk past me,
tail triumphantly erect. Clamped in its jaws was a discarded
fish-head, the prize from its successful foraging in the kitchen
refuse. It too was heading towards the Palazzo Farnese and the
banks of the Tiber beyond.